TOGETHER FOR LIFE®

FOR

CELEBRATING & LIVING THE SACRAMENT

TOGETHER
FOR
LIFE

SIXTH EDITION

JOSEPH M. CHAMPLIN
with PETER A. JARRET, C.S.C.

Contributors
Ann M. Garrido ~ Michael Heintz ~ Diana Macalintal
H. Richard McCord ~ Geoffrey D. Miller ~ Tim Muldoon
Julie Hanlon Rubio ~ William F. Urbine

AVE MARIA PRESS AVE Notre Dame, Indiana

Nihil Obstat: Reverend Mark Gurtner, JCL, *Censor Deputatis*

Imprimatur: Most Reverend Kevin C. Rhoades
                Bishop of Fort Wayne–South Bend
                November 2, 2011

Founded in 1865, Ave Maria Press is a ministry of the United States Province of Holy Cross.

www.avemariapress.com

Together for Life® is a registered trademark of Ave Maria Press, Inc.

Paperback: ISBN-13 978-1-64680-180-0

E-book: ISBN-13 978-1-64680-065-0

Cover image © Getty Images/Jupiter Images.

Cover and text design by Brian C. Conley.

Printed and bound in the United States of America.

Contents

Preface

Beginning in 1970, more than 9 million couples have used *Together for Life* to plan their weddings in the Catholic Church. That number accounts for nearly 80 percent of Catholic marriages in the United States in nearly five decades. The booklet's original author, Msgr. Joseph Champlin, a priest of the Diocese of Syracuse, wanted to strengthen and support Catholic marriages, and he believed that involving couples directly in planning for the liturgical celebration of their weddings was a good place to start. While taking a primary role in this planning is commonplace for engaged Catholic couples today, in 1970 it was quite a bold idea.

In the 1997 edition of *Together for Life*, Fr. Champlin wrote, "The Church recognizes that each of you is a unique individual and, together, form a unique couple. Consequently, it hopes you will actively plan and participate in a nuptial ceremony that will be distinctly your own, while still following a pattern standard for all Catholic weddings."

You now join the millions of couples who have used *Together for Life* to prepare their Catholic weddings. The hope and spirit of the book remain the same as they have always been even as new elements and new authors have been added over the years to better serve Catholic couples as the Church and our culture change and grow. Contributors now include priests, deacons, lay married theologians, and pastoral leaders from around the country who remain deeply committed to the sacramental life of the Church.

With a little work from both of you, your wedding ceremony will be a wonderful event for you as a couple, for your families and friends, and for the Church, which carries a deep hope and profound desire that your marriage will bloom and flourish as a sign of God's love in and for the world. Thank you for sharing your wedding day with the Church and for your witness of faith as you begin this wonderful new stage of your lives.

Peter A. Jarret, C.S.C.

Note to Priests, Deacons, and Other Parish Staff

Together for Life is designed for use in conjunction with the Ave Maria Press ritual cards edition of *The Order of Celebrating Matrimony* or as a stand-alone guide to help engaged couples plan a Catholic wedding. *Together for Life* uses codes to help couples choose and record various elements of the wedding. These codes appear in bold type, with a letter indicating the element (part of the liturgy) and the numeral indicating particular options. For example, on page 11, **A1** indicates that the prayer that follows is a Collect and is the first option a couple may choose. For parishes using *The Order of Celebrating Matrimony Ritual Cards Edition*, these letter-numeral codes correspond to that resource and help presiders match a couple's desired prayers, readings, formula of consent, and blessings to the ritual cards, which the presider then places in a ceremonial binder for use at the wedding.

The codes are straightforward for elements A–F, the Introductory Rites through the Liturgy of the Word. When couples reach the Celebration of Matrimony beginning on page 88, they will notice that the codes become more complex with the addition of (Form 1), (Form 2), and (Form 3). These terms correspond to the three forms of The Celebration of Matrimony described on pages 2 and 10 of this booklet: (1) Within Mass, (2) Without Mass, and (3) Between a Catholic and a Catechumen or a Non-Christian.

Couples need to know which form of the celebration will be used at their wedding in order to complete this section of *Together for Life*. Once known, they can simply follow the options coded for that form. We urge you to read the introduction to *The Order of Celebrating Matrimony*, particularly #33–#38, to learn the circumstances in which each form of the celebration is to be used.

In *The Order of Celebrating Matrimony Ritual Cards Edition*, the elements that make up the Celebration of Matrimony (the Questions before Consent through the Blessing of Rings, options G, H, and I) appear in their entirety under each form of the celebration even when the words to be spoken aloud are the same. Because of this, separate codes are listed for these elements in *Together for Life* to account for each form of the celebration. For example, on pages 90–91, the words of Consent under the First Formula are the same in all three forms of the celebration. The different codes are necessary for priests, deacons, or other parish personnel who use *The Order of Celebrating Matrimony Ritual Cards Edition* for weddings.

Using This Booklet

Planning your wedding day can seem like a daunting task, involving (as it does) a large number of people and a seemingly endless array of details. Often, in the midst of making plans for the reception, flowers, dresses, tuxedos, photographs, travel arrangements, and on and on, the wedding liturgy itself can begin to feel like "just one more thing" you have to do. But your wedding ceremony is the central part of your big day. It is a sacred celebration meant to express your faith in God and your love for each other. It is, in fact, what makes you married—legally, publicly, and in the eyes of the Church.

When you exchange your vows you publicly proclaim your unending love for each other and your intention to remain together for life. By doing so, the love you received as a gift from God becomes a gift to the whole Church and to the world. When the Church says marriage is a sacrament, it means that your visible love and faithfulness to each other become a witness and an effective sign of God's love and care for all people. Your marriage is a sacramental sign not just to each other, to family and friends, or to the Church, but also to the entire world.

With the help of *Together for Life*, we pray you will experience the planning of your wedding liturgy as a labor of love, one that draws the two of you together more deeply into the mystery of God's love. In that way, your own faith in God and in each other will be expressed in the prayers, readings, and blessings you select, and your wedding liturgy will be a wonderful beginning to your married life.

In the following pages, you will find a list of frequently asked questions with brief answers; an outline of the three forms of celebrating matrimony in the Catholic Church; and step-by-step instructions for choosing from the prayers, scripture readings, and blessings available to you.

Begin by reading through the frequently asked questions and their brief answers on pages 3–9. Some questions will not pertain to you, but many will. These will help answer questions regarding issues such as which of the three forms for celebrating matrimony you should use and whether your best man and maid/matron of honor need to be Catholic.

Together for Life is laid out in a way that explains each section of the wedding liturgy, from your entrance into the church as bride and groom to your recessional as husband and wife. In various sections you are given options from which to choose. This symbol 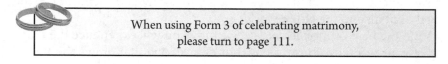 appears at the beginning of each of these sections so that you can easily see where you are asked to make a choice.

As you make each decision, record it on the selection form found at the back of this booklet or at **TogetherforLifeOnline.com**. As you work through the sections beginning with The Celebration of Matrimony on page 88, you will need to know which form of the rite you will use (see page 10).

Record each choice using both the letter-number code you see in the heading for each prayer, reading, or blessing and the page number on which your selection is found. Once you have completed your selection form, pass it on to the priest or deacon who will preside at your wedding.

There are three forms of celebrating matrimony: (1) Matrimony within Mass, (2) Matrimony without Mass, and (3) Matrimony between a Catholic and a Catechumen or a Non-Christian. The person helping you plan your wedding will guide you in choosing which form of the rite is most appropriate for your wedding. If you use either Form 2 or 3, you will not use pages 98–101 of this booklet, which pertain only to weddings celebrated within Mass (Form 1).

If you will be using Form 3 of the rite, you will be directed to move ahead so that you can make your selections for the concluding parts of your wedding ceremony. Look for the boxed notes like this one to guide you:

When using Form 3 of celebrating matrimony, please turn to page 111.

The appendixes at the end of this booklet offer information on celebrating marriage between a Catholic and a person who is not Catholic and incorporating cultural and ethnic traditions into your wedding celebrations while respecting the integrity of the Church's liturgy. All of these topics and many more are also addressed at **TogetherforLifeOnline.com**. As you begin your married life, we urge you to visit this site and **JoinedbyGrace.com** for more information about building a strong Christian marriage.

Frequently Asked Questions about the Celebration of Catholic Weddings

My fiancé and I hear the wedding ceremony being called different things. Which is correct: *ceremony*, *liturgy*, or *liturgical celebration?*

Any of these terms is accurate. *Ceremony* has a more universal meaning and is used in reference to both civil and religious wedding celebrations. A *liturgy* or *liturgical celebration* is quite exclusively a religious event. The word *liturgy* comes from a Greek term meaning "the work of the people." We use it in the Catholic Church to define our communal and regulated worship. By *regulated* we simply mean that Church laws and guidelines determine what can and should be done during these public times of worship.

You will also see the words *rite* and *order* used frequently in this booklet. These terms are used to define an established set of ritual words and actions that we use for particular liturgical celebrations. All of the sacraments, for example, are celebrated using specific rites or orders that have been written and formally approved for use in the Church.

We live in separate cities. Is it okay if one of us makes all the arrangements?

While it makes sense to divide up responsibilities for many of the details that go into your wedding day, it is important that you plan your wedding liturgy together as much as possible. Try to work together in choosing the readings, prayers, form of marriage vows, blessings, and music together. You will also want to talk about and decide the form of your entrance processional and recessional in conversation with parish personnel.

Can our wedding take place outdoors, in my parent's home, or at a restaurant?

Catholics are required to celebrate their wedding in a Catholic Church, before a priest and two witnesses. If the bride or groom is not Catholic and you wish for the wedding to take place in his or her church, or at some other location, that is possible with special permission of your home diocesan bishop. It is important to work through your local parish so that the requirements for the Catholic person are fulfilled.

Only one of us is Catholic. Can we still have Mass?

Yes, but it is worth thinking carefully about this. If you want to have Mass, you will need permission from your bishop to do so. The Church says that when either the bride or groom is not Catholic, the second or third form of the celebration (see page 10) should be used unless pastoral concerns suggest otherwise. The wedding ceremony should be as inclusive as possible, and if one of you cannot receive Communion or if you will have a large number of non-Catholic guests, it is preferable to use one of the forms without Mass.

For more information on marriage between a Catholic and a non-Catholic, please see appendix A (pages 114–116).

Is the wedding still a sacrament if there is no Mass?

The free exchange of consent (vows) between a baptized man and a baptized woman makes the marriage a sacrament, not the act of doing so within the context of a Mass. The Order of Celebrating Matrimony without Mass is just as valid a celebration of the sacrament as the Order of Celebrating Matrimony within Mass. However, if both bride and groom are Catholic, the normal form of celebrating matrimony is within Mass.

I know that we can be validly married in the Catholic Church, even though my fiancé has never been baptized. What will be different about our wedding ceremony?

The Order of Celebrating Matrimony between a Catholic and a Catechumen or a Non-Christian is similar to the other two forms of the marriage rite, but it will not contain language that pertains to sacrament, since only someone who is baptized receives sacraments. There will be prayers, readings, a blessing, and—most importantly—the exchange of consent or vows. You will not celebrate the Liturgy of the Eucharist or have Communion. As you work through this booklet, you will see notes directing you to the appropriate pages if you will be using this form of the celebration.

For more information on marriage between a Catholic and a non-Christian, please see appendix A (pages 114–116).

Will our non-Catholic family and friends be able to receive Communion if we do have Mass?

The Catholic Church understands the reception of Holy Communion to be the preeminent sign of unity among Christians. Sadly, divisions still exist within the church, and as a result of these divisions, inter-communion is not permitted. If one of you is not Catholic and if you will have a large number of non-Catholics guests, it is suggested that you do not have a Mass so that the issue of who may receive Communion and who may not does not become a source of disunity at your celebration.

For more information on this question, please see "A Pastoral Note on Inter-communion" on page 115.

Can the ordained minister from my fiancé's church have a role at our wedding?

Yes, with some restrictions. Take up the question with the priest or deacon who will preside at your wedding. In short, you must have one person who officially witnesses your marriage or receives your consent (vows), for legal reasons of both state and Church. In other words, your priest and your fiancé's minister or pastor cannot "co-officiate" using the Catholic rite, nor can they each celebrate their own ritual at your wedding. In certain circumstances, a minister from another church may proclaim a scripture reading, give an exhortation, or pray a blessing at a Catholic wedding so long as he or she has been invited to do so by the pastor of the Catholic parish.

Do our best man and maid/matron of honor both have to be Catholic?

No. According to the Canon Law of the Church, you need two witnesses in addition to the presider. You do not specifically need one man and one woman, and the witnesses do not need to be baptized. They do need to understand what is going on and so must have reached the age of reason and be in full control of their reason. For example, if one or both of your witnesses are intoxicated or otherwise impaired, they may not fill this role.

How many people should be involved in our wedding liturgy?

The Order of Celebrating Matrimony requires the bride and groom, a priest or deacon, and two witnesses (usually your best man and maid/matron of honor) be present. In addition to those essential participants, you will likely want to have one or more readers and a cantor and/or a musician to lead singing. You may also include others such as groomsmen and bridesmaids. You do not need a flower girl or ring bearer, but they may also be included, provided they are old enough to undertake the role you are giving them. Sometimes ushers are used to help seat your guests when they arrive at the church, and if you are celebrating with Mass, you may need people to bring the bread and wine forward and others to serve as extraordinary ministers of Holy Communion.

Do we have to sing?

It is customary to sing during Catholic worship, so check with the person helping you plan your wedding liturgy about the diocesan and parish expectations with regard to music and singing. He or she can assist you in choosing what will help and not hinder your celebration.

Can we choose any songs we want for our wedding?

The music chosen for your wedding must be commonly understood as sacred music. The Church has a rich tradition of beautiful hymns and other music from which you can choose what pieces you wish to use at your wedding with the guidance of your parish contact.

Where do we find musicians for the ceremony?

Check with the parish where your wedding will take place. If the parish staff does not include music ministers, they will often help you contact musicians and perhaps provide guidance on hiring them.

We've seen a variety of entrance processions at weddings. Is there a particular way we have to do this? What about the recessional?

The Order of Celebrating Matrimony calls for the bride and groom to be welcomed by the presiding priest or deacon at the doors of the church, similar to how we begin a baptism or the Rite of Welcome with those who want to join the Catholic Church. When this occurs, some couples choose to greet guests at the church entrance as a simple act of hospitality. The entrance procession then begins.

A second option is for the priest or deacon to go to the place where the bride and groom will be seated or he goes to his chair. When they have arrived at their place, he warmly greets the couple.

Various forms of the entrance procession are permissible as long as they conform to local guidelines. One option is to have a formal liturgical procession precede the wedding party, including cross and candle bearers, the reader, and the priest or deacon who will preside. Another option is to have the bridesmaids and groomsmen come in as couples with the bride and groom also processing as a couple and their parents preceding them. Or the bride can be accompanied by her parents and the groom by his. A father walking his daughter down the aisle to be given away is also a common element of the procession. While this was a fitting custom long ago, it may or may not be desirable for the two of you. Your parish contact can tell you what is permissible and help you determine what is most appropriate for your wedding.

May we use readings that are not in the Bible?

The Order of Celebrating Matrimony calls for the use of particular scripture readings as the primary way that God speaks to us about the nature and meaning of the sacrament. The options available for you to use at your Catholic wedding are presented in this booklet along with brief commentaries beginning on page 14. Poems and other readings not found in the Bible may not be used for your wedding liturgy, but consider using them as part of your rehearsal dinner or wedding reception.

May non-Catholics proclaim the readings during the liturgy?

If you choose to use the second or third form of the celebration, which do not include Mass, then yes. However, if you are having Mass, then a Catholic should proclaim the readings. In either situation, the readers should be trained in the ministry, well coached ahead of time in the church, and given time to practice with the microphone that will be used on your wedding day.

Who can be extraordinary ministers of Holy Communion?

The distribution of Holy Communion is a sacred moment in the liturgy. The local parish may have its own policy for extraordinary ministers, but if you are permitted to select extraordinary ministers of Communion, it is essential that they have already been trained.

Do we have to memorize our vows? Can we write our own vows?

While your vows are deeply personal, they are not private. Rather, they are public expressions of your love, faithfulness, and commitment. Couples are not free to write their own vows but may choose from options found on pages 90–92. Some priests or deacons suggest that couples memorize the vows while others do not.

Do we have to write our own intercessions?

You do not; depending on the liturgical norms of your parish and diocese, it is possible to write your own intercessions or use one of the forms given in this book, This is a question to which the priest or deacon who will preside at your wedding can best respond. Many couples start with one of the intercessions provided in this booklet and add names of deceased family members or friends to it. You may also add particular intentions that might be appropriate given your individual circumstances or a particular season of the year. Guidelines for composing your own intercessions—should you be free to do so—can be found at TogetherforLifeOnline.com.

Can we have a blessing of *arras*? Blessing and placing of the *lazo*?

The Order of Celebrating Matrimony contains two optional blessings: one for the *arras* and another for the *lazo*. The adaptations of these traditions—important for Hispanic and Filipino cultures—have already been approved for use in the United States in Spanish since 2010. Making them available in English translation is intended for occasions when one (or both) of the spouses has this cultural background and the couple wishes to celebrate their wedding in English.

For more information on these traditions visit TogetherforLifeOnline.com, Catholic Weddings, Catholic Wedding Traditions.

May we light a unity candle?

The unity candle is not part of the Catholic celebration of matrimony. The symbolism of "two becoming one" that the unity candle is meant to signify is already present with your exchange of vows and the blessing and exchange of rings. Many parishes ask that if you desire a unity candle, it be used at the rehearsal dinner or reception instead. As is the case with all customs that are not part of the official rite, it is best to speak about this with the priest or deacon who is presiding at your wedding.

For more information on including customs and traditions not part of the official rite, please see appendix B (pages 116–118).

Can we light a candle or do something in memory of a deceased parent?

Honoring those you love who cannot be present at your wedding is a fitting thing to do. For those who have a deceased parent or loved one, a candle lit in their memory or a special flower placed in the church is appropriate. It is also common to include a special remembrance of deceased loved ones in the Universal Prayer (Prayer of the Faithful).

Talk over your options for a memorial during the ceremony with the priest or deacon who will preside at your wedding.

Should we take flowers to a statue of Mary?

Although this custom is not part of *The Order of Celebrating Matrimony*, many couples who have a devotion to Mary want to take a moment at the conclusion of the liturgy to offer prayers to Mary as they begin their married life together. Mary is a wonderful model of how we are to live out our faith and trust in God. Couples will often bring flowers to the statue of Mary in the church and offer prayers asking for her intercession. This ritual usually takes place at the end of the ceremony. You may also be able to choose a Marian hymn such as the "Ave Maria" to be sung during this time.

Do we need a program or worship aid?

While it is not necessary, a program or worship aid will help your guests by providing musical refrains, prayer and reading responses, and an outline of the order of the ceremony. A handout will be especially helpful for those in attendance who are not familiar with Catholic liturgy. For information about reprinting the scripture readings visit usccb.org/bible/permissions.

Do we have to go to confession before our wedding?

One of the best ways for Catholics to prepare spiritually for their wedding day is to celebrate the sacrament of Penance or Reconciliation (i.e., go to confession). This may be a big step, especially if you have not been to confession in some time, but it is well worth talking this possibility over with the priest, deacon, sponsor couple, or other marriage preparation contact at the parish. Making time to examine your Christian commitments in confession prior to accepting your new role in the Church as a married person is a wonderful way to experience the healing, forgiveness, and grace Christ offers you.

Three Forms of Celebrating Matrimony

1. Within Mass	2. Without Mass	3. Between a Catholic and a Catechumen or a Non-Christian
Introductory Rites	*Introductory Rites*	*Rite of Reception*
Welcome	Welcome	Welcome
Procession	Procession	Procession
Gloria	Collect	
Collect		
Liturgy of the Word	*Liturgy of the Word*	*Liturgy of the Word*
Old Testament	Old Testament	One or two readings *at least one must explicitly speak of marriage
Responsorial Psalm	Responsorial Psalm	
New Testament	New Testament	
Gospel	Gospel	Homily
Homily	Homily	
Celebration of Matrimony	*Celebration of Matrimony*	*Celebration of Matrimony*
Introduction	Introduction	Introduction
Questions before Consent	Questions before Consent	Questions before Consent
Consent	Consent	Consent
Reception of Consent	Reception of Consent	Reception of Consent
Blessing and Giving of Rings [and *Arras*]	Blessing and Giving of Rings [and *Arras*]	Blessing and Giving of Rings [and *Arras*]
Universal Prayer/Prayer of the Faithful	Universal Prayer/Prayer of the Faithful [Lord's Prayer]	Universal Prayer/ Prayer of the Faithful
	[Blessing and Placing of the *Lazo* or Veil]	[Blessing and Placing of the *Lazo* or Veil]
	Nuptial Blessing	Nuptial Blessing
Liturgy of the Eucharist		
Preparation of the Altar	[Holy Communion]	
Eucharistic Prayer	Lord's Prayer	
Lord's Prayer	Sign of Peace	
[Blessing and Placing of the *Lazo* or Veil]	Communion	
Nuptial Blessing		
Sign of Peace		
Communion		
Prayer after Communion		
Conclusion of the Celebration	*Conclusion of the Celebration*	*Conclusion of the Celebration*
Solemn Blessing	Blessing	Blessing
Recessional	Recessional	Recessional

The Introductory Rites

The wedding liturgy begins with a welcome by the priest or deacon at the door of the church, followed by the entrance procession. Alternatively the greeting occurs after the bride and groom have entered and arrived at the places prepared for them. After all arrive in their places, they make the sign of the cross. The priest or deacon greets everyone at this point if this did not happen at the doors of the church. When Mass is celebrated the Gloria is said or sung. Then the Collect (cól-lect) is prayed. Please refer to the FAQs on pages 3–9 for more information about choosing a form of procession.

Collect

The Collect serves to gather the assembled community together in prayer. It helps unite all present in a bond of spiritual friendship and focuses their attention on the liturgical activity about to take place.

Please choose one of the following prayers and record it on your selection form, using the letter-number coding that appears as the heading of each prayer.

A1

The prayer A1 may not be used if the first Nuptial Blessing (M1) is selected.

> O God, who consecrated the bond of Marriage
> by so great a mystery
> that in the wedding covenant you foreshadow
> the Sacrament of Christ and his Church,
> grant, we pray, to these your servants,
> that what they receive in faith
> they may live out in deeds.

Through our Lord Jesus Christ, your Son,
who lives and reigns with you in the unity of the Holy Spirit,
one God, for ever and ever.

A2

O God, who in creating the human race
willed that man and wife should be one,
join, we pray, in a bond of inseparable love
these your servants who are to be united in the covenant of
    Marriage,
so that, as you make their love fruitful,
they may become, by your grace, witnesses to charity itself.
Through our Lord Jesus Christ, your Son,
who lives and reigns with you in the unity of the Holy Spirit,
one God, for ever and ever.

A3

Be attentive to our prayers, O Lord,
and in your kindness
pour out your grace on these your servants (N. and N.),
that, coming together before your altar,
they may be confirmed in love for one another.
Through our Lord Jesus Christ, your Son,
who lives and reigns with you in the unity of the Holy Spirit,
one God, for ever and ever.

A4

Grant, we pray, almighty God,
that these your servants,
now to be joined by the Sacrament of Matrimony,
may grow in the faith they profess
and enrich your Church with faithful offspring.
Through our Lord Jesus Christ, your Son,
who lives and reigns with you in the unity of the Holy Spirit,
one God, for ever and ever.

A5

Be attentive to our prayers, O Lord,
and in your kindness uphold
what you have established for the increase of the human race,
so that the union you have created
may be kept safe by your assistance.
Through our Lord Jesus Christ, your Son,
who lives and reigns with you in the unity of the Holy Spirit,
one God, for ever and ever.

A6

O God, who since the beginning of the world
have blessed the increase of offspring,
show favor to our supplications
and pour forth the help of your blessing
on these your servants N. and N.,
so that in the union of Marriage
they may be bound together
in mutual affection,
in likeness of mind,
and in shared holiness.
Through our Lord Jesus Christ, your Son,
who lives and reigns with you in the unity of the Holy Spirit,
one God, for ever and ever.

The Liturgy of the Word

In the scripture readings proclaimed during Catholic weddings, we hear of God's steadfast love for his people and of our call to make the whole of our lives a response to that love. It is a love story that began at creation and culminated in the death and resurrection of Jesus, God's only beloved Son. Through the gift of the Holy Spirit, the love of God poured out for us is made visible in the world. It is a love to which you will bear witness through the love you share as husband and wife.

After the scripture readings are proclaimed, the priest or deacon will deliver a homily based on the readings and on the Church's theology of marriage. The purpose of the homily is to help everyone present better understand the Word of God in the context of the celebration of marriage.

Choosing Your Readings

If you use the first or second form of the *Order of Celebrating Matrimony*, you will choose one reading from the Old Testament, a Responsorial Psalm, a reading from the New Testament, and a reading from one of the gospels. If you use the third form, you will choose one, two, or three readings. At least one reading must speak explicitly about marriage. These are marked with an asterisk after the letter-number combination.

Before the Gospel, an Alleluia or Gospel Verse is sung. For this and the Responsorial Psalm, you will work with the parish music director to learn which settings are available to you. Each scripture passage is followed in this booklet by a brief commentary called "The Word Brought Home" to help you in your selections.

Read through the readings and commentaries and choose which you want used for your wedding. Write your choices on the selection form, using the letter-number combination that appears in the heading for the reading. Also record the page number.

The number you see in parentheses is the lectionary number for that reading. The lectionary is the book of scripture readings we use for liturgical celebrations. This number will help your presider or his delegate mark the lectionary for your rehearsal and wedding.

Old Testament Readings

B1*
Genesis 1:26–28, 31a
(801-1)

Male and female he created them.

A reading from the Book of Genesis

Then God said:
"Let us make man in our image, after our likeness.
Let them have dominion over the fish of the sea,
        the birds of the air, and the cattle,
        and over all the wild animals
        and all the creatures that crawl on the ground."

God created man in his image;
        in the image of God he created him;
        male and female he created them.

God blessed them, saying:
        "Be fertile and multiply;
        fill the earth and subdue it.
Have dominion over the fish of the sea, the birds of the air,
        and all the living things that move on the earth."
God looked at everything he had made, and he found it very good.

The word of the Lord.

The Word Brought Home

This reading from the book of Genesis affirms what the two of you already know—that the creative and procreative energy of self-giving love is an incredible force for good. People and institutions in every age have believed the body—and sex in particular—to be a human frailty to be wary of, to be dealt with only in hushed whispers, or to be treated as explicitly evil. The two of you certainly do not feel that way. Your love is very special, a beautiful experience—probably the most wonderful thing that has happened so far in your life. Deep down you must be thinking that anything so good must come from God. And you are right.

People have been reading this biblical passage from Genesis for thousands of years. The words and message are clear: we came forth from God's creative hand and are fashioned in the divine image and likeness. God, who made our minds, our hearts, and our bodies, finds us and all his creation "very good."

From the beginning God blessed man and woman with the power of bringing forth new life and the charge of being good stewards of the earth. When as husband and wife you cooperate with God to create a new person, you will do so by sharing the most intimate parts of yourselves: physically, emotionally, and spiritually. Maintaining a healthy, satisfying sex life can be hard work, and it demands of both spouses an ongoing commitment to the good of the other and to the good of the marriage. Parenthood can be even harder. Family life requires patience, hard work, and above all, self-sacrificing love.

This reading from the story of creation serves as a reminder that you do not face this future alone. God who created you and who invites you to share in the awesome power of creating new life also promises to stand by you. Be confident that the Lord who is love and creator of all that is good will be with you always and in every effort.

B2*   The two of them become one body.
Genesis 2:18–24
(801-2)

A reading from the Book of Genesis

The Lᴏʀᴅ God said: "It is not good for the man to be alone.
I will make a suitable partner for him."
So the Lᴏʀᴅ God formed out of the ground
    various wild animals and various birds of the air,
    and he brought them to the man to see what he would call them;
    whatever the man called each of them would be its name.
The man gave names to all the cattle,
    all the birds of the air, and all wild animals;
    but none proved to be the suitable partner for the man.

So the Lᴏʀᴅ God cast a deep sleep on the man,
    and while he was asleep,
    he took out one of his ribs and closed up its place with flesh.
The Lᴏʀᴅ God then built up into a woman the rib
    that he had taken from the man.
When he brought her to the man, the man said:

"This one, at last, is bone of my bones
    and flesh of my flesh;
This one shall be called 'woman,'
    for out of 'her man' this one has been taken."

That is why a man leaves his father and mother
    and clings to his wife,
    and the two of them become one body.

The word of the Lord.

The Word Brought Home

"This one, at last!" Adam cries out in wonder and gratitude when God brings Eve to him. Each of us probably felt something similar when we realized we were completely in love with the person we wanted to marry. What an awesome discovery to find a person who—just like Adam encountering Eve—we knew to be a "suitable partner." We felt so grateful and completely alive. This was the one, at last!

In this reading and in the one immediately preceding it, the biblical author teaches us two important truths about men and women. The first truth is that men and women are created equal as persons. Together, in their maleness and femaleness, they convey the full image of God.

In the second creation account, found in Genesis 2:4–25 and from which this reading is taken, we learn the second, equally great truth. Men and women are created as different persons specifically as part of the divine plan. They are made to be male and female precisely so they can live for each other in the totality of their lives and truly be gifts to each other. Their differences, which are rooted in their sexuality, serve to unite them. Their differences are complementary, certainly in a physical sense but also in the many ways that men and women relate as equal and distinct persons.

In marriage, these two great truths—the equality of persons and the necessity of both sexes—together flourish as a foundational part of God's plan for humanity. When Adam says that Eve is "bone of my bones and flesh of my flesh" he is using an expression that, in effect, means "we are made of the same stuff." In other words, we are equal as human beings. But, at the same time, Adam makes it clear that he has discovered in the woman a different person to whom he can "cling" and with whom he can "become one body."

Affirming these two truths about equality and difference is fundamental to finding happiness and true fulfillment in married life. Why? Because expressing them in concrete actions is what enables us to make a complete gift of self to our spouse and, at the same time, to receive our spouse totally as a gift. This mutual giving and receiving is what you pledge in the wedding vows.

Will you be a gift that keeps on giving once the wedding is over and the years of married life begin to unfold? At times, you will find it difficult to fully accept your spouse as a gift and also to give yourself as a gift. It is important to remember that because God brought you together for a purpose, he will surely give you the strength to accomplish that purpose. In the years to come, try to recall that moment when, like Adam, you thought, "At last, this is the one for me!" Hold fast to the joy of your discovery and cherish each other.

B3*

Genesis 24:48–51, 58–67

(801-3)

In his love for Rebekah, Isaac found solace after the death of his mother.

A reading from the Book of Genesis

The servant of Abraham said to Laban:
    "I bowed down in worship to the LORD,
        blessing the LORD, the God of my master Abraham,
        who had led me on the right road
        to obtain the daughter of my master's kinsman for his son.
    If, therefore, you have in mind to show true loyalty to my master,
        let me know;
        but if not, let me know that, too.
    I can then proceed accordingly."
Laban and his household said in reply:
    "This thing comes from the LORD;
    we can say nothing to you either for or against it.
Here is Rebekah, ready for you;
    take her with you,
    that she may become the wife of your master's son,
    as the LORD has said."

So they called Rebekah and asked her,
    "Do you wish to go with this man?"
She answered, "I do."
At this they allowed their sister Rebekah and her nurse to take leave,
    along with Abraham's servant and his men.
Invoking a blessing on Rebekah, they said:

    "Sister, may you grow
        into thousands of myriads;
    And may your descendants gain possession
        of the gates of their enemies!"

Then Rebekah and her maids started out;
    they mounted their camels and followed the man.
So the servant took Rebekah and went on his way.

Meanwhile Isaac had gone from Beer-lahai-roi
    and was living in the region of the Negeb.
One day toward evening he went out . . . in the field,
    and as he looked around, he noticed that camels were approaching.
Rebekah, too, was looking about, and when she saw him,
    she alighted from her camel and asked the servant,
    "Who is the man out there, walking through the fields toward us?"
"That is my master," replied the servant.

Then she covered herself with her veil.

The servant recounted to Isaac all the things he had done.
Then Isaac took Rebekah into his tent;
    he married her, and thus she became his wife.
In his love for her Isaac found solace
    after the death of his mother Sarah.

The word of the Lord.

The Word Brought Home

The story of Isaac's marriage to Rebekah seems worlds apart from the way most people in our part of the world think about marriage. It is a story from the ancient Near East, a world governed by rules about clan, bloodline, and household. Peering past the differences of four thousand years, we can see five themes from this story that help us think about marriage today.

1. *Marriage affects the extended family.* Abraham sent his servant on a long journey to find a wife for his son Isaac. He understood that it was important for his son to marry a woman who shared his beliefs so that they would carry on the covenant with God. Marriage brings families together— sometimes from greatly divergent cultures— because two people discover a deep bond to which they are called to say yes.

2. *Marriage affects the entire community.* In the biblical story, both Isaac and Rebekah are from wealthy families, and so their marriage is in some ways like a royal wedding today, impacting all those who are part of the clan. Even for ordinary couples, marriage will have an impact on the way they relate to a wider community. Decisions about where to live, where and when to work, how to spend free time and money, where to send children to school, and so on grow out of married life. Marriage has a ripple effect throughout a church, a neighborhood, and even a nation.

3. *Marriage is something God does.* Most prominent in the story is the idea that God has a hand in leading Abraham's servant to Rebekah and in helping Laban see that "this thing comes from the Lord." Our Catholic tradition carries forward this ancient insight, believing that marriage is created by God as a particular way of building a kingdom of love and justice.

4. *Marriage is a vocation.* We use the term vocation (or "calling") as a way of talking about our response to what God is doing through us. Laban's words reveal that he recognizes that God is the author of the story and that we are all actors in it. We reach our joy and freedom by saying yes to the calling of God moving in our lives.

5. *Marriage is a solace,* a comfort. The closing lines of the story point to how we understand the meaning of vocation: it is God's way of moving us toward love. Isaac, grieved by his mother's death, finds solace in Rebekah. And while the story—like much ancient literature of the Middle East— focuses more on the male characters, we can imagine that Rebekah's willingness to meet Isaac meant that she, too, found great consolation. We call that consolation *grace*— God's free gift of love that enables wives and husbands to love each other through all the comforts and challenges of life.

B4*

Tobit 7:6–14
(801–4)

**May the Lord of heaven prosper you both.
May he grant you mercy and peace.**

A reading from the Book of Tobit

Raphael and Tobiah entered the house of Raguel and greeted him.
Raguel sprang up and kissed Tobiah, shedding tears of joy.
But when he heard that Tobit had lost his eyesight,
    he was grieved and wept aloud.
He said to Tobiah:
    "My child, God bless you!
You are the son of a noble and good father.
But what a terrible misfortune
    that such a righteous and charitable man
    should be afflicted with blindness!"
He continued to weep in the arms of his kinsman Tobiah.
His wife Edna also wept for Tobit;
    and even their daughter Sarah began to weep.

Afterward, Raguel slaughtered a ram from the flock
    and gave them a cordial reception.
When they had bathed and reclined to eat,
    Tobiah said to Raphael, "Brother Azariah,
    ask Raguel to let me marry my kinswoman Sarah."
Raguel overheard the words;
    so he said to the boy:
    "Eat and drink and be merry tonight,
    for no man is more entitled to marry my daughter Sarah
    than you, brother.
Besides, not even I have the right to give her to anyone but you,
    because you are my closest relative.
But I will explain the situation to you very frankly.
I have given her in marriage to seven men,
    all of whom were kinsmen of ours,
    and all died on the very night they approached her.
But now, son, eat and drink.
I am sure the Lord will look after you both."
Tobiah answered, "I will eat or drink nothing
    until you set aside what belongs to me."

Raguel said to him: "I will do it.
She is yours according to the decree of the Book of Moses.
Your marriage to her has been decided in heaven!
Take your kinswoman;

from now on you are her love,
and she is your beloved.
She is yours today and ever after.
And tonight, son, may the Lord of heaven prosper you both.
May he grant you mercy and peace."
Then Raguel called his daughter Sarah, and she came to him.
He took her by the hand and gave her to Tobiah with the words:
"Take her according to the law.
According to the decree written in the Book of Moses she is your wife.
Take her and bring her back safely to your father.
And may the God of heaven grant both of you peace and prosperity."
He then called her mother and told her to bring a scroll,
so that he might draw up a marriage contract
stating that he gave Sarah to Tobiah as his wife
according to the decree of the Mosaic law.
Her mother brought the scroll,
and he drew up the contract,
to which they affixed their seals.

Afterward they began to eat and drink.

The word of the Lord.

The Word Brought Home

Applying an ancient text to our current situation is often difficult, but this reading offers valuable lessons for young couples today.

Notice the importance of family in this scene. Both of Sarah's parents are involved in some fashion. Her father, Raguel, formally hands her in marriage to Tobiah and blesses the young couple, and her mother, Edna, helps prepare materials for the marriage contract.

Today, many couples embark on their new life together by themselves, as if their prior relationships must now take a back seat. Tobiah and Sarah show us that this new relationship does not mean we discard old ones. Rather, married life has a communal dimension. Love is meant to be shared, and a healthy marriage is one where the love of two people radiates outward, spreading love to others and receiving love in return.

Although strange to our world view, Tobiah's desire to marry his blood relative would have been commonplace in ancient Israel. Marrying someone of the same family or clan helped to ensure that people remained committed to the Lord and to the religious precepts of Judaism. In our modern religiously pluralistic society, this concern is not as prevalent. Catholics who marry non-Catholics can still display a robust faith.

Regardless of creed, we should keep in mind that each of us is ultimately seeking union with God. A successful marriage, like all relationships, is one where we help each other come closer to that goal. This is a great challenge for us, for we are called to inspire our beloved spouse and to embody God's love for him or her. It is comforting to know that this person whom we hold dear is doing the same for us.

B5*

Tobit 8:4b–8
(801–5)

Allow us to live together to a happy old age.

A reading from the Book of Tobit

On their wedding night Tobiah arose from bed and said to his wife,
    "Sister, get up. Let us pray and beg our Lord
    to have mercy on us and to grant us deliverance."
Sarah got up, and they started to pray
    and beg that deliverance might be theirs.
They began with these words:

    "Blessed are you, O God of our fathers;
        praised be your name forever and ever.
    Let the heavens and all your creation
        praise you forever.
    You made Adam and you gave him his wife Eve
        to be his help and support;
        and from these two the human race descended.
    You said, 'It is not good for the man to be alone;
        let us make him a partner like himself.'
    Now, Lord, you know that I take this wife of mine
        not because of lust,
        but for a noble purpose.
    Call down your mercy on me and on her,
        and allow us to live together to a happy old age."

They said together, "Amen, amen."

The word of the Lord.

The Word Brought Home

The first thing that the newlyweds do in this reading from the book of Tobit is pray. This may seem odd, but in fact you will marry within a liturgical celebration of the Church filled with prayer and blessing.

In the biblical story, Tobiah and Sarah have just married and her parents have escorted them to the bridal chamber to spend their first night together. Before retiring for the evening, Tobiah asks his wife to pray with him, and then together they ask the Lord to bless their union. Tobiah and Sarah provide a great example for all newly married couples looking to start their marriage off on the right foot. A good marriage is one where the spouses invite God to play an active role in their lives and to nourish and sustain them for years to come.

Of course, making time for prayer is not always easy. This is true when you are single, and it is even truer when you add another person's schedule, daily concerns, and your mutual need to be together into the mix. Once children enter the picture, your lives can be easily caught up with play dates, soccer practices, piano lessons, and the like. Suddenly your busyness has left little room for prayer. Wise spouses will try to imitate Tobiah and Sarah and pray together, thanking God for his bountiful goodness and asking for his continued blessings. In a successful marriage, communication is a top priority, not only with your spouse but also with your heavenly Father, from whom all good things come.

Although they've only been married for a few hours, Tobiah and Sarah are already thinking like a couple. They pray that deliverance be theirs, that God show mercy on both of them, and that they be allowed to live together to a happy old age. Tobiah likens himself and his wife to Adam and Eve, whom God created to be true partners for each other. The Hebrew word for "partner" is *neged*, which means a relationship of equality, harmony, and cooperation. The transition to this new reality can be hard for anyone to make, especially since modern society values individualism so very highly. But being married does not mean that the husband and wife totally extinguish the self; rather, you now enter into a new reality that transcends your individual identity. As spouses you are joined in an unbreakable bond and live in a new kind of partnership. You no longer pursue two distinct paths conjointly but walk the same path together. All the intimacies and details of daily life belong not to you alone but are shared.

The prayer of Sarah and Tobiah demonstrates a healthy understanding of what it means to walk the same path together. In good times and in bad, may you remember their example and together take your gratitude and need before our faithful God.

B6*   She who fears the LORD is to be praised.

Proverbs 31:10–13, 19–20, 30–31
(801–6)

A reading from the Book of Proverbs

When one finds a worthy wife,
  her value is far beyond pearls.
Her husband, entrusting his heart to her,
  has an unfailing prize.
She brings him good, and not evil,
  all the days of her life.
She obtains wool and flax
  and makes cloth with skillful hands.
She puts her hands to the distaff,
  and her fingers ply the spindle.
She reaches out her hands to the poor,
  and extends her arms to the needy.
Charm is deceptive and beauty fleeting;
  the woman who fears the LORD is to be praised.
Give her a reward of her labors,
  and let her works praise her at the city gates.

The word of the Lord.

The Word Brought Home

The book of Proverbs, written about six centuries before the birth of Jesus, captures the lived wisdom of the people of Israel and their neighbors. It offers practical advice and warnings about how to handle the ups and downs of life, how to raise children, how to conduct business, and how to run a fruitful household. The book closes with the passage we find here on the rich blessing of a "worthy wife," or a wife of great worth.

The passage presents a fascinating glimpse into the life of a woman in a wealthy household in ancient Israel: She is engaged in the many tasks involved in managing her own family's life, but she is also involved in the marketplace and in selling things outside her home. Moreover, she is involved in charitable activity, reaching out to those in need. This woman is clearly creative, hardworking, and engaged in the larger community. She sounds not unlike many of the women and men that we encounter every day.

Work is a central feature in every family's life. Catholic social teaching highlights that the creation of a healthy, happy home is naturally a priority of married couples but that, in the end, families are not solely about themselves and their own flourishing. Families are called, through their work in the marketplace and their charitable activities, to also serve the greater good. They are called to be agents of transformation in the world.

One of the biggest challenges any contemporary family faces is finding the right balance among work in the home, work outside of the home, and church or civic engagement. Different couples handle this challenge in various ways. Not long ago, it was common for women to take responsibility for work in the home, men to take responsibility for work outside the home, and one or both to engage in some sort of larger civic engagement. There is nothing sacrosanct, however, about this arrangement. Other cultures and other periods of time have worked out alternative arrangements very successfully.

Who will be responsible for which household tasks in your new home? Do you each plan on having an outside job or maintaining a career? Will one person's job take priority over the other's? How will your household contribute to the bettering of the larger community? How do you hope to manage parenting roles and responsibilities? No couple has every question resolved as they begin their marriage, and truly they cannot. Things change, shifting your hopes and dreams and all your careful planning. Even so, respectfully honoring the dignity of work—both the tasks of household management and your outside jobs—and valuing the contributions both of you make will help you find deep reward in your labors.

B7   Stern as death is love.

Song of Songs 2:8–10, 14, 16a; 8:6–7a
(801–7)

A reading from the Song of Songs

Hark! my lover—here he comes
    springing across the mountains,
    leaping across the hills.
My lover is like a gazelle
    or a young stag.
Here he stands behind our wall,
    gazing through the windows,
    peering through the lattices.
My lover speaks; he says to me,
    "Arise, my beloved, my dove, my beautiful one, and come!

"O my dove in the clefts of the rock,
    in the secret recesses of the cliff,
Let me see you,
    let me hear your voice,
For your voice is sweet,
    and you are lovely."

My lover belongs to me and I to him.
    He says to me:

"Set me as a seal on your heart,
    as a seal on your arm;
For stern as death is love,
    relentless as the nether-world is devotion;
    its flames are a blazing fire.
Deep waters cannot quench love,
    nor floods sweep it away."

The word of the Lord.

The Word Brought Home

The Song of Songs (or Canticle of Canticles or Song of Solomon) is a beautiful love poem attributed to Solomon, the king of Israel in the tenth century BC. It was probably actually written a few centuries later. Its highly erotic language made some early commentators wonder whether it really belonged in the Bible at all, especially since there is no mention of God and its imagery is rather explicitly sexual. In light of these facts, it is particularly interesting to consider how Rabbi Akiba, who was writing just a few decades after the time of Jesus, thought about this poem. He saw it as absolutely central to the meaning of the whole of scripture because it is the story of hearts on fire for love.

In the Jewish tradition, the Song of Songs is read during the season of Passover, the season that recollects the story of God leading Israel out of Egypt toward the Promised Land. Passover recalls the hardships of the Jewish people as they wandered homeless in the desert. It seems perhaps an odd time to introduce the theme of erotic love. But the rabbis, in their wisdom, understood that it was this kind of powerful love that led God to reach out to Israel: the story of love is the inner story that celebrates the outer story of the Exodus from Egypt. God so loved the nation of Israel that he was willing to rescue it and bring it home, even when its love for God faltered.

It is interesting for Christians to consider, in light of this rabbinic reading, how Jesus' suffering and death—the Passion—took place during the Passover celebration. The word *passion* comes from a Latin verb that means "to suffer," and this idea makes sense when we think about what love entails.

Passionate love is a single-minded devotion to the object of one's desire, to the extent that one is willing to take on any hardship for the sake of that love. Think about Romeo and Juliet or Tristan and Isolde—classic stories of lovers sacrificing everything out of love.

Early in many relationships, the experience of passionate love is surprising, enthralling, and overwhelming. It can be confusing, then, when ordinary life circumstances make it hard to sustain that feeling. Jobs, financial issues, concerns about family or home—all these things take our energy and time away from the all-encompassing feeling of passion.

The author of the First Letter of John tells us that God is love (4:8). St. Augustine suggests we seek first not a feeling we associate with love but rather to know God and find our love in knowing him. A spouse is, in the Catholic understanding of marriage, the sacrament or sacred sign of God's love for us. Over time the passion, the feelings, will arise in ever-deepening ways from that love.

B8*   Like the sun rising in the LORD's heavens,

Sirach 26:1-4, 13-26 (Vg 26:1–4,16–21) the beauty of a virtuous wife is the

(801–8)   radiance of her home.

A reading from the Book of Sirach

Blessed the husband of a good wife,
    twice-lengthened are his days;
A worthy wife brings joy to her husband,
    peaceful and full is his life.
A good wife is a generous gift
    bestowed upon him who fears the LORD;
Be he rich or poor, his heart is content,
    and a smile is ever on his face.

A gracious wife delights her husband,
    her thoughtfulness puts flesh on his bones;
A gift from the LORD is her governed speech,
    and her firm virtue is of surpassing worth.
Choicest of blessings is a modest wife,
    priceless her chaste soul.
A holy and decent woman adds grace upon grace;
    indeed, no price is worthy of her temperate soul.
Like the sun rising in the LORD's heavens,
    the beauty of a virtuous wife is the radiance of her home.

The word of the Lord.

The Word Brought Home

How can we know we have found the right one? In other times and places people married for more practical reasons, but today most of us want to marry our "soulmate." The writer of the book of Sirach was a second-century BC Jewish teacher who counseled his male students to value character over all else when choosing a wife. If he were teaching today, he might add warnings about the fleeting nature of romance, and he would likely talk about character as something that is important to seek in both husbands and wives.

But what is good character? Between the verses shown in this reading, there are verses where the author of the book of Sirach describes the vices of a really bad wife: she is envious, angry, prone to drunkenness, lustful, headstrong, and impulsive. In contrast, this excerpt shows that a virtuous wife is humble, slow to anger, faithful, disciplined enough to run an orderly home, and full of grace.

But is a spouse with good character enough to sustain a marriage? One contemporary theologian likes to scandalize his students by saying, "You always marry the wrong person." He does not mean to discourage them from getting to know someone well before proposing marriage, but we cannot know everything about someone. People change over time. Economic, cultural, and religious realities change, too. We simply cannot anticipate serious illness, job loss, infertility, or other struggles that we or our children might face. At times, a spouse may seem to be "the wrong person"—one whose interests, ideas, or temperament do not match up with ours. Yet if we have chosen well, his or her good character will be a source of grace in the good times when we feel blessed and in the bad times when we have to stretch to be the person our spouse deserves.

Two people of strong character come together in Christian marriage not simply to pursue a romance but also to build a life. Together they create a home and a rhythm of living centered around people rather than material things. Together they decide how to prioritize commitments to marriage, work, children, elders, the neighborhood, schools, and the community. Together they make their home a place of peace, joy, and welcome.

Sirach's vision is not quite as romantic as soulmates who fall in love at first sight and know they will always be together in blissful tranquility. But if we choose a person of good character to marry, perhaps, like the husband in this passage, we will be grateful to have by our side a really good person, a partner whose faithful presence is as beautiful as "the sun rising in the LORD's heavens."

B9

Jeremiah 31:31–32a, 33–34a

(801–9)

I will make a new covenant with the house of Israel and the house of Judah.

A reading from the Book of the Prophet Jeremiah

> The days are coming, says the LORD,
>> when I will make a new covenant with the house of Israel
>> and the house of Judah.
> It will not be like the covenant I made with their fathers:
>> the day I took them by the hand
>> to lead them forth from the land of Egypt.
> But this is the covenant which I will make
>> with the house of Israel after those days, says the LORD.
> I will place my law within them, and write it upon their hearts;
>> I will be their God, and they shall be my people.
> No longer will they have need to teach their friends and relatives
>> how to know the LORD.
> All, from least to greatest, shall know me, says the LORD.

The word of the Lord.

The Word Brought Home

Many of the agreements people make are conditional transactions: "I'll do this if you do that." In this system, rules are central. Following them ensures harmony. It is the way society functions and does business. But it is not the best way to treat the promises we make in marriage.

The prophet Jeremiah reminded the people of Israel that being in a relationship with God was more than just about following rules. It was about remembering to whom one belonged. In the Old Covenant, God gave rules in the Ten Commandments and in the Law of Moses. But time and time again, the people broke them and turned to other gods. Yet as many times as the Israelites were unfaithful, God always called them back. His desire for his people was so great that God made a new promise, one based not on rules but on love. In this New Covenant, God promised to be with them, no matter what. God would never forget his own, and in response to this unconditional love, God's people would remember that they belonged to God.

This New Covenant, then, would need only one rule, one that would not need to be taught because God's people would change from the inside out. The New Covenant would be written on their hearts so they could not forget it.

No matter how much you love each other, there will come times in your relationship when you will fall short. It is simply the reality of being human. There will be little mistakes now and then. There may be big ones, too. Making a promise or a covenant cannot prevent this, but it does give you hope.

If you can remember that you belong to each other and to God, there will always be hope for healing. If you can remember the things that first drew you to each other, there can be hope for a new beginning. If you can remember that your life together means that you are no longer alone, that you belong to another in love, then you can work through whatever challenges you will face together. You need not rely on a list of rules. Instead, you can rely on your love for each other and on God's love for you.

As you prepare to make your promises to each other, let your hearts be open so that God can write his law upon them. Savor the memories you have created with each other, and write those on your hearts each day.

Just as God has made a covenant with you so too does the Church. You belong to us, and we belong to you. We will not always be perfect, but we will always strive to remember the promise we make to you on your wedding day to love you no matter what and to help you remember that God does the same.

Responsorial Psalms

C1   The goodness of the Lord.

Psalm 33:12 and 18, 20–21, 22
(803–1)

Response: The earth is full of the goodness of the Lord.

Blessed the nation whose God is the Lord,
    the people he has chosen as his heritage.
Yes, the Lord's eyes are on those who fear him,
    who hope in his merciful love.
The earth is full of the goodness of the Lord.

Our soul is waiting for the Lord.
    He is our help and our shield.
In him do our hearts find joy.
    We trust in his holy name.
The earth is full of the goodness of the Lord.

May your merciful love be upon us,
    as we hope in you, O Lord.
The earth is full of the goodness of the Lord.

C2   Bless the Lord.

Psalm 34:2–3, 4–5, 6–7, 8–9
(803–2)

Response: I will bless the Lord at all times.
or: Taste and see the goodness of the Lord.

I will bless the Lord at all times,
    praise of him is always in my mouth.
In the Lord my soul shall make its boast;
    the humble shall hear and be glad.
I will bless the Lord at all times.
or: Taste and see the goodness of the Lord.

Glorify the Lord with me;
    together let us praise his name.
I sought the Lord, and he answered me;
    from all my terrors he set me free.
I will bless the Lord at all times.
or: Taste and see the goodness of the Lord.

Look toward him and be radiant;
    let your faces not be abashed.

This lowly one called; the Lᴏʀᴅ heard,
    and rescued him from all his distress.
I will bless the Lord at all times.
or: Taste and see the goodness of the Lord.

The angel of the Lᴏʀᴅ is encamped
    around those who fear him, to rescue them.
Taste and see that the Lᴏʀᴅ is good.
    Blessed the man who seeks refuge in him.
I will bless the Lord at all times.
or: Taste and see the goodness of the Lord.

C3   The Lord is kind and merciful.

Psalm 103:1–2, 8 and 13, 17–18a
(803–3)

Response: The Lord is kind and merciful.
or: The Lord's kindness is everlasting to those who fear him.

Bless the Lᴏʀᴅ, O my soul,
    and all within me, his holy name.
Bless the Lᴏʀᴅ, O my soul,
    and never forget all his benefits.
The Lord is kind and merciful.
or: The Lord's kindness is everlasting to those who fear him.

The Lᴏʀᴅ is compassionate and gracious,
    slow to anger and rich in mercy.
As a father has compassion on his children,
    the Lᴏʀᴅ's compassion is on those who fear him.
The Lord is kind and merciful.
or: The Lord's kindness is everlasting to those who fear him.

But the mercy of the Lᴏʀᴅ is everlasting
    upon those who hold him in fear,
upon children's children his righteousness,
    for those who keep his covenant.
The Lord is kind and merciful.
or: The Lord's kindness is everlasting to those who fear him.

C4   Blessed is the man.

Psalm 112:1bc-2, 3–4, 5–7a, 7bc–8, 9
(803–4)

**Response: Blessed the man who greatly delights in the Lord's commands.
or: Alleluia.**

Blessed the man who fears the LORD,
    who takes great delight in his commandments.
His descendants shall be powerful on earth;
    the generation of the upright will be blest.
**Blessed the man who greatly delights in the Lord's commands.
or: Alleluia.**

Riches and wealth are in his house;
    his righteousness stands firm forever.
A light rises in the darkness for the upright;
    he is generous, merciful, and righteous.
**Blessed the man who greatly delights in the Lord's commands.
or: Alleluia.**

It goes well for the man who deals generously and lends,
    who conducts his affairs with justice.
He will never be moved;
    forever shall the righteous be remembered.
He has no fear of evil news.
**Blessed the man who greatly delights in the Lord's commands.
or: Alleluia.**

With a firm heart, he trusts in the LORD.
With a steadfast heart he will not fear;
    he will see the downfall of his foes.
**Blessed the man who greatly delights in the Lord's commands.
or: Alleluia.**

Openhanded, he gives to the poor;
    his righteousness stands firm forever.
    His might shall be exalted in glory.
**Blessed the man who greatly delights in the Lord's commands.
or: Alleluia.**

C5*   Blessed are those who fear the Lord

Psalm 128:1–2, 3, 4, 5ac and 6a
(803–5)

> Response: Blessed are those who fear the Lord.
> or: See how the Lord blesses those who fear him.

Blessed are all who fear the LORD,
    and walk in his ways!
By the labor of your hands you shall eat.
    You will be blessed and prosper.
> Response: Blessed are those who fear the Lord.
> or: See how the Lord blesses those who fear him.

Your wife like a fruitful vine
    in the heart of your house;
your children like shoots of the olive
    around your table
> Response: Blessed are those who fear the Lord.
> or: See how the Lord blesses those who fear him.

Indeed thus shall be blessed
    the man who fears the LORD.
May the LORD bless you from Zion
    all the days of your life!
    May you see your children's children.
> Response: Blessed are those who fear the Lord.
> or: See how the Lord blesses those who fear him.

C6   The Lord is compassionate.

Psalm 145:8–9, 10 and 15, 17–18
(803–6)

> Response: How good is the Lord to all.

The LORD is kind and full of compassion,
    slow to anger, abounding in mercy.
How good is the LORD to all,
    compassionate to all his creatures.
> Response: How good is the Lord to all.

All your works shall thank you, O LORD,
    and all your faithful ones bless you.
The eyes of all look to you,
    and you give them their food in due season.
> Response: How good is the Lord to all.

The LORD is righteous in all his ways,
    and holy in all his deeds.
The LORD is close to all who call him,
    who call on him in truth.
Response: How good is the Lord to all.

C7   Praise the Lord.

Psalm 148:1–2, 3–4, 9–10, 11–13a, 13c–14a
(803–7)

    Response: Let all praise the name of the Lord.
    or: Alleluia.

Praise the LORD from the heavens;
    praise him in the heights.
Praise him, all his angels;
    praise him, all his hosts.
Response: Let all praise the name of the Lord.
or: Alleluia.

Praise him, sun and moon;
    praise him, all shining stars.
Praise him, highest heavens,
    and the waters above the heavens.
Response: Let all praise the name of the Lord.
or: Alleluia.

Mountains and all hills,
    fruit trees and all cedars,
beasts, both wild and tame,
    creeping things and birds on the wing.
Response: Let all praise the name of the Lord.
or: Alleluia.

Kings of the earth and all peoples,
    princes and all judges of the earth,
young men and maidens as well,
    the old and the young together.
Let them praise the name of the LORD,
    for his name alone is exalted.
Response: Let all praise the name of the Lord.
or: Alleluia.

His splendor above heaven and earth.
> He exalts the strength of his people.

Response: Let all praise the name of the Lord.
or: Alleluia.

New Testament Readings

D1   What will separate us from the love of Christ?

Romans 8:31b–35, 37–39
(802–1)

A reading from the Letter of Saint Paul to the Romans

Brothers and sisters:
If God is for us, who can be against us?
He did not spare his own Son
    but handed him over for us all,
    will he not also give us everything else along with him?
Who will bring a charge against God's chosen ones?
It is God who acquits us.
Who will condemn?
It is Christ Jesus who died, rather, was raised,
    who also is at the right hand of God,
    who indeed intercedes for us.
What will separate us from the love of Christ?
Will anguish, or distress, or persecution, or famine,
    or nakedness, or peril, or the sword?
No, in all these things, we conquer overwhelmingly
    through him who loved us.
For I am convinced that neither death, nor life,
    nor angels, nor principalities,
    nor present things, nor future things,
    nor powers, nor height, nor depth,
    nor any other creature will be able to separate us
    from the love of God in Christ Jesus our Lord.

The word of the Lord.

The Word Brought Home

A priest walked outside one Sunday during Mass and came upon a couple outside the building's main entrance. The young man was holding a young child in his arms and comforting his pregnant wife who was sitting on the steps, covering her face with her hands. The heat and crowd combined with morning sickness had made her feel faint and dizzy. This gentle scene more accurately mirrors the real world of marriage than any dreamy, trouble-free portrait sketched by romanticists.

Weddings are and should be occasions filled with joy and laughter, bright promise, faith and hope, and profound affection—but also with a fair amount of sobering realism. The union to which you consent with your marriage vows holds many yet-to-be-discovered ups and downs, joys and struggles. Yet here you are saying yes to that vast mysterious life that is Christian marriage. Your future stretches before you in exciting images of hope and with probably at least some trepidation. Just what that future holds you will discover together, side by side, keeping each other company through it all.

This reading from the letter of St. Paul to the Romans reminds us that, come what may, Christ Jesus will be with us as well. This was true for the early Christians who suffered persecution and martyrdom because of their beliefs, and it is just as true for the two of you and for all of us today. Life will bring you pain and sorrow, but these cannot tear you away from God. As long as your love for Christ remains strong, you can cling to him and to each other through even your darkest times.

Real love, as St. Paul reminds us, is stronger than death. The husband and wife who truly love each other need fear neither death nor life, neither anything that exists nor anything still to come. Their death-defeating, cross-conquering mutual love will merely grow through afflictions.

A crucifix in your new home can be a constant reminder of these truths. It tells of Jesus' suffering, his victory, and his love for us. It speaks of the share every couple must have in the Lord's death and resurrection. It reminds us that, with love for Christ and for each other, nothing can come between us.

D2

Romans 12:1–2, 9–18 *or* 12:1–2, 9–13
(802–2)

For the short form, omit bracketed text.

Offer your bodies as a living sacrifice, holy and pleasing to God.

A reading from the Letter of Saint Paul to the Romans

I urge you, brothers and sisters, by the mercies of God,
    to offer your bodies as a living sacrifice,
    holy and pleasing to God, your spiritual worship.
Do not conform yourselves to this age
    but be transformed by the renewal of your mind,
    that you may discern what is the will of God,
    what is good and pleasing and perfect.

Let love be sincere;
    hate what is evil,
    hold on to what is good;
    love one another with mutual affection;
    anticipate one another in showing honor.
Do not grow slack in zeal,
    be fervent in spirit,
    serve the Lord.
Rejoice in hope,
    endure in affliction,
    persevere in prayer.
Contribute to the needs of the holy ones,
    exercise hospitality.

[Bless those who persecute you,
    bless and do not curse them.
Rejoice with those who rejoice,
    weep with those who weep.
Have the same regard for one another;
    do not be haughty but associate with the lowly;
    do not be wise in your own estimation.
Do not repay anyone evil for evil;
    be concerned for what is noble in the sight of all.
If possible, on your part, live at peace with all.]

The word of the Lord.

The Word Brought Home

It is dangerous to imagine that you can reform or fix a future spouse. You truly are committing to love and stick by this person forever, warts and all. Even so, people do change—usually for the better—after falling in love and continuing to grow in that love. Couples, just like friends, influence one another and many times bring out the best in each other. Other relationships and life experiences will also cause each of you to change as you mature in your marriage.

Teenagers infatuated with a first love may start to think about another's needs before their own for the first time in their lives. They buy each other gifts and call or text with each other for hours. They learn about romantic love and about how happiness can come from getting out of oneself and thinking about another first.

The two of you left that tender, important, but premature love behind long ago. Yours is presumably a more secure, lasting type of love that has the happiness of the other as its goal. Your prime desire is to make each other happy, but this may only be possible if you open your hearts to the outside world and become concerned about the well-being and happiness of the other people around you.

In this reading from the letter of St. Paul to the Romans, we find wonderful coaching for creating a marriage that is hospitable to the wider community in which you will live. Paul instructs his fellow Christians to rejoice in hope, endure in affliction, and persevere in prayer; in other words, to build a strong bond between the two of you. He urges you and all of us to care for and welcome others, to "bless" those who do you harm, and to be empathetic, or keep company, with both those who rejoice and those who weep. He urges you not to seek revenge or return one bad deed with another and not to think too highly of yourself. Perhaps the most difficult piece of advice for spouses to remember when married life gets strained is Paul's advice to treat one another with the same hospitality that we would welcome from others.

We need have no fears. Welcoming, loving, and caring for others outside the family; giving in the right way; and being involved in other people's lives will not harm the love between husband and wife. When you first loved your partner, you gave, but in the giving, you gained more. As a couple, your love and giving to those outside the home will enable your own love to grow stronger and deeper. Our God is faithful and keeps the promises he has made to us.

D3   Welcome one another as Christ welcomed you.

Romans 15:1b–3a, 5–7, 13

(802–3)

A reading from the Letter of Saint Paul to the Romans

Brothers and sisters:
We ought to put up with the failings of the weak and not to please
      ourselves;
      let each of us please our neighbor for the good,
      for building up.
For Christ did not please himself.
May the God of endurance and encouragement
      grant you to think in harmony with one another,
      in keeping with Christ Jesus,
      that with one accord you may with one voice
      glorify the God and Father of our Lord Jesus Christ.

Welcome one another, then, as Christ welcomed you,
      for the glory of God.
May the God of hope fill you with all joy and peace in believing,
      so that you may abound in hope by the power of the Holy Spirit.

The word of the Lord.

The Word Brought Home

Invitations have been sent or will be sent soon. You are looking forward to welcoming many people at your wedding. Friends may be flying in from across the country, and relatives you have not seen for a while, or maybe do not know very well, are looking forward to the happy day. You are in a hospitable mood now and hopefully will continue that same spirit throughout your married life. Over the years to come, you will welcome extended family, friends, neighbors, and your children into your home and your married life. You will also learn the fine craft of welcoming your spouse in ever more intimate ways—gently honoring the other's vulnerabilities, fears, and faults and carefully accepting them just as they are on the really big days as well as in the incidental moments.

This reading from St. Paul's letter to the Romans urges you to welcome others "for the glory of God." But what does that mean, for the glory of God? Perhaps the best way to explain this in this context is to say that the glory of God refers to God's deepest, innermost, most essential identity. It is hard to characterize God with human attributes, but that is as close as we can come. Consequently, for Paul to say that welcoming others glorifies God, he means that in authentically welcoming others we give outward expression to the essence of God. What then is the essence of God? In Catholic theological thought, the outward, spiraling love that exists among the three persons of the Trinity is the essence of God for God *is* love. By welcoming one another we glorify or make known the essence of God to those around us.

Becoming a welcoming couple comes from your experiences of hospitality up to this point. Learning to be graceful and accept others into your married life will be both exciting and challenging. Your attention in the coming weeks will be on planning the wedding and preparing a home for yourselves as husband and wife, but becoming a welcoming couple and family is a lifetime adventure together.

Welcoming each other as husband and wife means being open to the growth that will occur in each other. It means accepting and learning to love each other's quirks and annoying habits along with the things you really like. Of course, one of the best and most challenging gifts of marriage is the welcoming of children. Nothing quite changes your life like becoming a parent or a stepparent. As children grow, so must parents.

God is indeed glorified—his innermost being revealed—in the hospitality shown between spouses and by married couples to those with whom they interact every day. Set your hearts on this, then, so that you may know peace and joy and hope eternal: "Welcome one another, as Christ welcomed you."

D4

1 Corinthians 6:13c–15a, 17–20
(802–4)

Your body is a temple of the Spirit.

A reading from the first Letter of Saint Paul to the Corinthians

Brothers and sisters:
The body is not for immorality, but for the Lord,
    and the Lord is for the body;
    God raised the Lord and will also raise us by his power.

Do you not know that your bodies are members of Christ?
Whoever is joined to the Lord becomes one spirit with him.
Avoid immorality.
Every other sin a person commits is outside the body,
    but the immoral person sins against his own body.
Do you not know that your body
    is a temple of the Holy Spirit within you,
    whom you have from God, and that you are not your own?
For you have been purchased at a price.
Therefore glorify God in your body.

The word of the Lord.

The Word Brought Home

Even in this digital age, it is hard to imagine being satisfied with an exclusively virtual relationship. Plenty of people meet online and even get to know each other through technology, but inevitably they want to meet in person. To put it simply: there is something about physical presence that cannot be replaced.

Paul's observations about the body are not primarily about issuing criticisms of people who take their bodies for granted. He is calling attention to something that God has done: given us the gift of life through the gift of the body. Our bodies are "members of Christ," meaning that they are caught up in the same mystery of God becoming flesh that Christians celebrate in the Eucharist.

For Paul, the body was sacred. The human body of Jesus was the place where God became most immediately present to people. God had been present through his prophets and through the scriptures, which gave Israel a law and a way of life. But in Jesus Christ, God made people see that the human body is, in the words of St. Augustine, "capable of God"—that is, capable of manifesting the reality of God.

Paul's exhortations to the church at Corinth, then, were about helping them to realize how followers of Jesus should regard their bodies. There were some, it seemed, who wanted to say that bodies no longer mattered since in death we will no longer need bodies. But Paul observed that if bodies didn't matter, God would not have raised Jesus from the dead.

Theologians reflecting on the gospels centuries later came to an important understanding, one that has shaped Christian doctrine about Jesus ever since. They described the Incarnation—the "taking flesh" that the Holy Spirit accomplished in Mary's womb—as Jesus' being fully human and fully divine. What this means is that everything human, including our bodies, is sacred and able to be a vessel for God. It is no surprise, then, that Paul urges the Corinthians to "glorify God in your body." Far from a critique, this is a wonderful opportunity!

Though sometimes we may get the sense that our bodies are just bundles of tissue seeking stimuli (from things such as chocolate, wine, or sex), Paul suggests that our bodies can make us saints. Our bodies can comfort a friend with a hug, show concern for an elderly relative with a gentle touch, and help a newborn baby know that she is safe. Perhaps most surprisingly, Paul points to an idea at the root of marriage: our sexual bodies can heal the loneliness of the other and even, at certain times, bring forth new life.

By being joined to Christ, our bodies become the ways in which Christ himself touches others in love. Let us pray, then, that all our desires—those of our minds, our hearts, and even our bodies—might glorify God.

D5

1 Corinthians 12:31–13:8a
(802–5)

If I do not have love, I gain nothing.

A reading from the first Letter of Saint Paul to the Corinthians

Brothers and sisters:
Strive eagerly for the greatest spiritual gifts.

But I shall show you a still more excellent way.

If I speak in human and angelic tongues
    but do not have love,
       I am a resounding gong or a clashing cymbal.
And if I have the gift of prophecy
    and comprehend all mysteries and all knowledge;
    if I have all faith so as to move mountains,
    but do not have love, I am nothing.
If I give away everything I own,
    and if I hand my body over so that I may boast
    but do not have love, I gain nothing.

Love is patient, love is kind.
It is not jealous, is not pompous,
    it is not inflated, it is not rude,
    it does not seek its own interests,
    it is not quick-tempered, it does not brood over injury,
    it does not rejoice over wrongdoing
    but rejoices with the truth.
It bears all things, believes all things,
    hopes all things, endures all things.
Love never fails.

The word of the Lord.

The Word Brought Home

St. Paul wrote this famous passage on love for the Christian community of Corinth in the middle of the first century. Founded only a few years earlier, the Corinthian church enjoyed only a brief honeymoon before finding itself embroiled in a number of contentious issues that threatened to disintegrate its union. The attraction among the members faded to the point that they had a hard time breaking bread with one another. Paul wanted to wean them away from the notion of love as feeling and to remind them that mature love is an act of the will. Love may begin with an intense desire to be with one another, but if it is to last, it will require a series of daily behaviors that sustain and deepen the relationship—like being patient and kind and not being jealous, pompous, inflated, rude, or selfish. Love, as Paul writes, endures all things. What a claim he makes!

We all know that there is an almost irresistible attraction between partners as they fall in love that is absolutely necessary for nourishing the budding relationship—just as necessary as milk is to an infant. We can hardly stand to be apart. Our bodies hunger for the touch of the other. Our minds percolate in the presence of the other. Laughter comes more readily; hearts beats faster. The attraction knits us together as a couple and helps us to grow. It is the beginning of love, and the energy is incredibly powerful.

But as time goes on, attraction can wax and wane. Our wider culture—which often conflates attraction and love—perceives this change as a danger. If we no longer *feel* the same intense attraction toward each other, it must mean something is wrong or even that the marriage is over. In reality, however, it may simply mean that the relationship has matured to the point where it no longer needs attraction to bind it together. While attraction remains good and desirable in marriage, ultimately, love is not a feeling but an act of the will.

When mutual love matures and the almost frantic attraction of the first days eases, a husband and wife may find it less necessary to speak, to touch, and to look for chances to connect emotionally, physically, or spiritually. They may no longer seek eagerly to communicate in the same ways that they needed to at the outset. Connecting and loving come in subtler and yet deeper ways.

Consider your relationship. You are likely somewhere between the frenzy of new love and the maturity of many years together. Neither of you is likely to consistently live up to all of St. Paul's descriptions of love in this reading. But you are so very blessed because marriage is a school for the maturing of love if we allow it to be. Every day it gives us the chance to practice virtue and overcome vices. Welcome with confidence the many shades and seasons of love, for—as St. Paul reminds us—love endures.

D6   One Body and one Spirit

Ephesians 4:1–6
(807–2)

A reading from the Letter of Saint Paul to the Ephesians

Brothers and sisters:
I, a prisoner for the Lord,
    urge you to live in a manner worthy of the call you have received,
    with all humility and gentleness, with patience,
    bearing with one another through love,
    striving to preserve the unity of the Spirit
    through the bond of peace: one Body and one Spirit,
    as you were also called to the one hope of your call;
    one Lord, one faith, one baptism;
    one God and Father of all,
    who is over all and through all and in all.

The word of the Lord.

The Word Brought Home

Paul urges the Christians in Ephesus to "live in a manner worthy of the call they have received." Often, we tend to associate having a "call" with a vocation to the religious life or priesthood. But *all* of us have a vocation. *All* of us are called. The question is, *called to what?*

At a most fundamental level, all of us are called to happiness—which from a Christian perspective is *always* found in the joy of being in relationship with and service to others. Because each of us is unique, the form that happiness will take varies. Indeed, it varies greatly. The particular ways that we like to relate, the particular works we enjoy, the particular passions that drive us differ. But, in the words of the preacher Frederick Buechner in *Wishful Thinking,* "The place God calls you to is the place where your deep gladness and the world's deep hunger meet."

For many, marriage is an important part of the vocational journey. It is not for everyone. Some find that living singly or in some other form of community life is a better fit for them given their personality and sense of mission. But across generations and cultures, many have found that marriage is the particular form of life that best molds them into the people God dreams them to be. Marriage sands their rough edges and makes them grow in virtues like patience, humility, gentleness. It offers a means to render service in the world. Marriage is not a lesser call, nor is it a superior call. But it is, as St. Paul tells us, a *worthy* call.

The problem, as Paul notes, is that many of us do not live our lives, including our marriages, out rooted in a sense of vocation. We tolerate our jobs, our spouses, our children instead of seeing them as part of how God is helping us grow as persons. We grow weary of the mundane details of house repairs and meal preparation and carpooling rather than looking at how these tasks might fit into God's larger plan of service. But every time we make a choice to bear with one another and strive to preserve a spirit of unity and peace with one another in the midst of our daily lives, it is a sign of our commitment to live life intentionally rather than just as a reaction to one thing after another. This intentional living is a sign of our commitment to live in a manner befitting the beautiful worthiness of our calls.

D7

Ephesians 5:2a, 21–33 *or*
5:2a, 25–32
(802–6)
For the short form, omit bracketed text.

This is a great mystery, but I speak in reference to Christ and the Church.

A reading from the Letter of Saint Paul to the Ephesians

Brothers and sisters:
Live in love, as Christ loved us
    and handed himself over for us.

[Be subordinate to one another out of reverence for Christ.
Wives should be subordinate to their husbands as to the Lord.
For the husband is head of his wife
    just as Christ is head of the Church,
    he himself the savior of the body.
As the Church is subordinate to Christ,
    so wives should be subordinate to their husbands in everything.]

Husbands, love your wives,
    even as Christ loved the Church
    and handed himself over for her to sanctify her,
    cleansing her by the bath of water with the word,
    that he might present to himself the Church in splendor,
    without spot or wrinkle or any such thing,
    that she might be holy and without blemish.
So also husbands should love their wives as their own bodies.
He who loves his wife loves himself.
For no one hates his own flesh
    but rather nourishes and cherishes it,
    even as Christ does the Church,
    because we are members of his Body.
        For this reason a man shall leave his father and his mother
            and be joined to his wife,
        and the two shall become one flesh.
This is a great mystery,
    but I speak in reference to Christ and the Church.

[In any case, each one of you should love his wife as himself,
    and the wife should respect her husband.]

The word of the Lord.

The Word Brought Home

This reading causes many winks, elbow nudges, and rolling of eyes when people hear it in church. Hearing that a wife should be subordinate to her husband because he is her "head" doesn't fit with our twenty-first-century sensibilities or with our grasp of what makes a healthy marriage. But as with all biblical texts, we need to accept that this letter was written for a group of Christians that belonged to a different time and culture than we do. The passage actually points to a quite radical code of household behavior that marked the early Christian communities: husbands and wives were to be "subordinate to one another out of reverence for Christ." In other words, there was to be mutual serving and giving over to the needs of the other in order to show the world who Christ was.

The deeply entrenched social order of the day certainly left husbands in positions of authority to which their wives did not have access, and St. Paul was not trying to change that basic order. But that does not mean that the Bible calls Christians to follow the same culture-bound pattern today. Rather, Paul was trying to tell his readers that their households should be marked by a new code of conduct, a new way of living as married couples: he called them to mutual respect and love. Both of these would have been as strange to his listeners as the text seems to us today at first read. This was a quite radical teaching then. It was a new way for men to be heads of their households, yes, but it was also a new way for women to exist in the home—as mutually responsible for the well-being of the marriage and the household. For both husbands and wives to be called to partnership was indeed a new reality, a distinctively Christian way of being married.

So what does mutuality in marriage look like, and how does that kind of union become a sign or sacrament of God's love in the world? One way to think about it is through the lens of a small ritual action we see each time we go to Mass. As the priest readies the bread and wine for the Eucharistic Prayer, he pours just a bit of water into the chalice and prays in silence, "By the mystery of this water and wine, may we come to share in the divinity of Christ who humbled himself to share in our humanity." Drops of water disappear into wine. The two mix and become one. This holy co-mingling symbolizes a mysterious blending of the divine and human in Jesus Christ. In this simple action, we glimpse Christ as a kind of marriage between God and us, between the spiritual and the material, between this world and the next. By joining your lives together in Christ, your relationship and your marriage also become a sign of the unity of heaven and earth and of the unending love of God for all creation.

D8   The God of peace will be with you.

Philippians 4:4–9
(802–7)

A reading from the Letter of Saint Paul to the Philippians

Brothers and sisters:
Rejoice in the Lord always.
I shall say it again: rejoice!
Your kindness should be known to all.
The Lord is near.
Have no anxiety at all, but in everything,
    by prayer and petition, with thanksgiving,
    make your requests known to God.
Then the peace of God that surpasses all understanding
    will guard your hearts and minds in Christ Jesus.

Finally, brothers and sisters,
    whatever is true, whatever is honorable,
    whatever is just, whatever is pure,
    whatever is lovely, whatever is gracious,
    if there is any excellence
    and if there is anything worthy of praise,
    think about these things.
Keep on doing what you have learned and received
    and heard and seen in me.
Then the God of peace will be with you.

The word of the Lord.

D9   And over all these put on love,
                             that is, the bond of perfection.

Colossians 3:12–17
(802–8)

A reading from the Letter of Saint Paul to the Colossians

Brothers and sisters:
Put on, as God's chosen ones, holy and beloved,
    heartfelt compassion, kindness, humility, gentleness, and patience,
    bearing with one another and forgiving one another,
    if one has a grievance against another;
    as the Lord has forgiven you, so must you also do.
And over all these put on love,
    that is, the bond of perfection.
And let the peace of Christ control your hearts,
    the peace into which you were also called in one Body.

And be thankful.
Let the word of Christ dwell in you richly,
    as in all wisdom you teach and admonish one another,
    singing psalms, hymns, and spiritual songs
    with gratitude in your hearts to God.
And whatever you do, in word or in deed,
    do everything in the name of the Lord Jesus,
    giving thanks to God the Father through him.

The word of the Lord.

The Word Brought Home

We seek peace with all our hearts, but it often eludes us. We are forever trying to establish, sustain, or restore it within ourselves, in our relationships, and throughout our world. Knowing our desires, Jesus offers peace as his final gift to us. On the night before he died he told his disciples, "Peace I leave with you; my peace I give to you" (Jn 14:27).

In these two scripture readings St. Paul writes to communities that are not entirely at peace. Not long after Christ's ascension into heaven, his gift has already begun to slip through the grasp of his followers. They are challenged from the outside by persecution, but there is also dissension from within over certain beliefs and practices. So Paul instructs them about restoring and maintaining peace within their relationships. He tells them simply, "Keep on doing what you have learned and received and heard and seen in me. Then the God of peace will be with you."

Paul's instructions are just as relevant to married couples today as they were to the early Christian communities. Because conflict is a part of every marriage, peace-making is a necessity. Marital therapists say that most couples fight about the same things: finances, children, family relationships, and balancing home and work responsibilities. Why do these conflicts lead to marital breakdown for some but not for others? The difference between success and failure lies not in what couples fight about but rather in how they handle those inevitable conflicts.

In your marriage preparation you probably received practical advice about conflict resolution and communications skills to help you deal with the problems and tensions that arise in married life. It is important to learn how to "fight fair" and to distinguish between conflicts that can be solved and those that can only be managed. These are skills you can learn in order to "let the peace of Christ control your hearts" in married life. They can also be the foundation of a marriage built on the Christian virtues of compassion, kindness, gentleness, patience, and forgiveness.

A virtue is a habitual way of acting. It is a disposition toward what is good. It is a choice we make to open ourselves to God's love and become instruments of that love in our daily actions. By acquiring and practicing virtues, we follow the path to Christian holiness. Each virtue is a specific expression of love, which itself sums up all the virtues. So as you begin your journey of married love, decide to build your relationship on these Christian virtues. Then you will experience "the peace into which you were also called," especially when conflict arises.

D10   Let marriage be held in honor by all.
Hebrews 13:1–4a, 5–6b
(802–9)

A reading from the Letter to the Hebrews

Brothers and sisters:
Let mutual love continue.
Do not neglect hospitality,
      for through it some have unknowingly entertained angels.
Be mindful of prisoners as if sharing their imprisonment,
        and of the ill-treated as of yourselves,
        for you also are in the body.
Let marriage be honored among all
        and the marriage bed be kept undefiled.
Let your life be free from love of money
        but be content with what you have,
        for he has said, *I will never forsake you or abandon you.*
Thus we may say with confidence:

        The Lord is my helper,
        and I will not be afraid.

The word of the Lord.

The Word Brought Home

In thinking of hospitality, most of us imagine something like the perfectly manicured living rooms on a home decor website or someone like Martha Stewart and her enterprise of "good things." Or maybe you picture the greeter at the doors of the local megastore. But what does the letter to the Hebrews mean when it advises us to not neglect hospitality?

Biblical hospitality is essentially about helping others, especially strangers, get to where they need to be on their journey. Travel in ancient times was often a risky endeavor, and travelers depended on the kindness of those they met along the way for food, shelter, and rest before they continued on to their destination. In some cultures, people were obligated to invite travelers into their homes and offer them refreshment. In the course of this exchange, the host would also discover the travelers' purpose and destination and give them some gift that would help them along their way. In return, the guests promised to bring no harm to the home of the host. Not only did this keep travelers safe but it also ensured the good of the community.

The story in the book of Genesis of Abraham and Sarah, who invited three travelers into their home and fed them with the best they had to offer, is a good example of this system of hospitality. These three visitors turned out to be God's angels, and it was not the host couple but rather the angels who gave the gift. They brought the happy news to the elderly Abraham and Sarah that Sarah would bear a son—one who would continue their family line and eventually lead to another couple: Mary and Joseph and their son Jesus. In a real way, these angels disguised as strangers helped Abraham and Sarah get to where they needed to be—patriarch and matriarch of the line of David from which Jesus Christ was born.

To offer hospitality, then, is to bring blessing to others so they can be who they are meant to be. This kind of hospitality continues what God first did for humankind when he created the heavens and the earth. God didn't just make a place for us to survive; he made a place where we could thrive and become the people God intended us to be.

Hospitality that enables people to thrive enables them to feel comfortable and at home, helps them discover their destination or destiny, and supports them on their way there. To put it simply, hospitality is creating sacred space for another. When this becomes our goal, then all the other concerns of homemaking—issues of money, possessions, and parenting—fall into place.

As you make your home together, attend to the ways you create sacred space for each other and for those who come to you on their journey. May your home—and everywhere you spend time together—become a place of blessing where friends and strangers alike become their best and truest selves.

D11*

1 Peter 3:1–9
(802–10)

Be of one mind, sympathetic, loving toward one another.

A reading from the first Letter of Saint Peter

Beloved:
You wives should be subordinate to your husbands so that,
     even if some disobey the word,
        they may be won over without a word by their wives' conduct
     when they observe your reverent and chaste behavior.
Your adornment should not be an external one:
     braiding the hair, wearing gold jewelry, or dressing in fine clothes,
     but rather the hidden character of the heart,
     expressed in the imperishable beauty
     of a gentle and calm disposition,
        which is precious in the sight of God.
For this is also how the holy women who hoped in God
     once used to adorn themselves
     and were subordinate to their husbands;
        thus Sarah obeyed Abraham, calling him "lord."
You are her children when you do what is good
     and fear no intimidation.

Likewise, you husbands should live with your wives in understanding,
     showing honor to the weaker female sex,
     since we are joint heirs of the gift of life,
     so that your prayers may not be hindered.

Finally, all of you, be of one mind, sympathetic,
     loving toward one another, compassionate, humble.
Do not return evil for evil, or insult for insult;
     but, on the contrary, a blessing, because to this you were called,
     that you might inherit a blessing.

The word of the Lord.

The Word Brought Home

The original intention of the author of this reading can easily be lost in assumptions and debates about gender roles. Some interpret 1 Peter and similar New Testament texts as advocating limited roles for women and men as preordained by God. These texts have even been used to justify violence, especially against women who have refused to be "subordinate." There are, of course, richer strains of meaning for couples to mine in this text, otherwise the Church would not offer it for use at your wedding.

This reading offers an interesting glimpse into Christian communities trying to figure out their relationship with the larger world in the late first century. The passage suggests that many early Christian women were in marriages with non-Christians. That is what the author means in the opening lines about some husbands "disobeying the word." These women were in positions of little influence within the patriarchal structure of ancient Roman society, but rather than believe themselves to be powerless, the author of the letter challenges them to model virtue and service in such a way that their husbands will be "won over" to the Christian faith. Similar to maxims in Matthew's gospel regarding "going the extra mile" or "turning the other cheek," the author coaches these women to spread the Gospel by being just a bit subversive. Precisely by living in harmony with their spouses and modeling kindness, respect, and peaceable relationships, these women could show their husbands the way to Christ. This passage is not advocating that the patriarchal social ordering of the ancient world be followed today but rather it is saying that modeling Christian living is the best way to invite others to follow Christ.

There will likely be many times in your marriage when you feel trapped between a rock and a hard place. These times might come about because of an unwelcome job change, an unanticipated pregnancy, a grave diagnosis, a natural disaster, or a pattern of behavior that you see as problematic but your spouse does not. Peter's words in this reading remind us that even in circumstances where we seem to have no escape, we can still choose how we face the difficulty. We can choose to handle the hard times with grace, patient endurance, and creative problem solving or with grumbling, self-pity, and passivity. This freedom to choose can never be taken away from us, and our Christian calling demands that we choose to act in love.

How do you as individuals and as a couple respond to adversity? Do you assume a certain powerlessness, or do you seek creative ways to make your situation better? Are you, as the author of 1 Peter coaches, "of one mind, sympathetic toward one another, compassionate, humble," and are you able to return insult with blessing? In other words, do your behaviors toward each other and those around you—especially in hardship—model Christian living and provide others with a glimpse of Christ Jesus?

D12   Love in deed and in truth.
1 John 3:18–24
(802–11)

A reading from the first Letter of Saint John

Children, let us love not in word or speech
    but in deed and truth.

Now this is how we shall know that we belong to the truth
    and reassure our hearts before him
    in whatever our hearts condemn,
      for God is greater than our hearts and knows everything.
Beloved, if our hearts do not condemn us,
    we have confidence in God
    and receive from him whatever we ask,
      because we keep his commandments and do what pleases him.
And his commandment is this:
    we should believe in the name of his Son, Jesus Christ,
    and love one another just as he commanded us.
Those who keep his commandments remain in him, and he in them,
    and the way we know that he remains in us
    is from the Spirit that he gave us.

The word of the Lord.

D13   God is love.
1 John 4:7–12
(802–12)

A reading from the first Letter of Saint John

Beloved, let us love one another,
    because love is of God;
    everyone who loves is begotten by God and knows God.
Whoever is without love does not know God, for God is love.
In this way the love of God was revealed to us:
    God sent his only-begotten Son into the world
    so that we might have life through him.
In this is love:
    not that we have loved God, but that he loved us
    and sent his Son as expiation for our sins.
Beloved, if God so loved us,
    we also must love one another.

No one has ever seen God.
Yet, if we love one another, God remains in us,
    and his love is brought to perfection in us.
The word of the Lord.

The Word Brought Home

Soon you will stand before family, friends, and the Church's representative to face each other, join hands, and promise to share your lives together. This is a permanent commitment to love and honor in good times and in bad, in poverty and in plenty, in sickness and in health, for better or for worse. These are serious words and solemn vows—too serious and too solemn, perhaps, for some in our modern world.

Demographics show us that fewer and fewer people in the developed world get married and that, when they do, close to half of them divorce. Many people ask, "Why marry? Why not simply live together? Why commit yourself to anything more binding than a mutual agreement, a promise to maintain a living-together relationship only so long as it remains acceptable to both partners?" This argument has a certain logic. After all, why should couples who are no longer compatible wage a daily battle against each other and end up destroying each other? But it has a major weakness also.

A great part of the joy of an engagement and a marriage is the sense of security that goes with it; a feeling of being loved, wanted, and needed; and a realization that someone cares for you on a permanent basis. Only in the stress and strain of a permanent commitment does the real character of each person develop. The love and responsibilities demanded by such an enduring promise supply an opportunity for the full depth of a relationship between husband and wife to materialize. Authentic intimacy, depth of character, and profound, self-giving love develop in couples only with the long and steady flow of years, weathering together the storms of life, and cherishing the good times with joyful celebration.

All of this is dull, impractical, and unrealistic talk for the two of you in love! Your marriage will never fail; your love, never waver; and your commitment, never be questioned. In these blissful but sometimes blind days of courtship, you naturally think only in terms of forever. However, the alarming divorce rate, the talk about temporary commitments, and the lack of support in our culture for the preservation of marriage should make you approach your marriage with eyes wide open. A marriage that lasts for life demands hard work, faithfulness, good humor, and gentle kindness. Remaining together for life requires that you cling to God's grace, peace, and enduring love.

D14

Revelation 19:1, 5–9a
(802–13)

Blessed are those who have been called to the wedding feast of the Lamb.

A reading from the Book of Revelation

I, John, heard what sounded like the loud voice
of a great multitude in heaven, saying:

"Alleluia!
Salvation, glory, and might belong to our God."

A voice coming from the throne said:

"Praise our God, all you his servants,
    and you who revere him, small and great."

Then I heard something like the sound of a great multitude
    or the sound of rushing water or mighty peals of thunder,
    as they said:
    "Alleluia!
The Lord has established his reign,
    our God, the almighty.
Let us rejoice and be glad
    and give him glory.
For the wedding day of the Lamb has come,
    his bride has made herself ready.
She was allowed to wear
    a bright, clean linen garment."
(The linen represents the righteous deeds of the holy ones.)

Then the angel said to me,
    "Write this:
    Blessed are those who have been called
    to the wedding feast of the Lamb."

The word of the Lord.

The Word Brought Home

The book of Revelation describes the fall of Babylon as a triumph of God's justice over oppression and greed. The word "alleluia" appears in the New Testament only in Revelation 19, in celebration of God's justice and deliverance. Redemption and healing have come to God's people. When the author of Revelation tries to describe what God's reign looks like, he uses the image of a wedding banquet. Like the writer of the letter to the Ephesians (5:23–32), the author sees marriage as a revelation of God's love to humanity.

Revelation is a book of prophecy, but it also offered words of encouragement to the early Christians. The author says that "the good deeds of the saints" make up the dress of the bride of Christ. The goodness of Christians makes the Church ready to become the bride of Christ. With the unity of the Lamb and the Christian community, the reign of God has begun.

So, too, with the union of any bride and groom, the reign of God comes a little closer. Justice, deliverance, redemption, and healing are made visible in the calling together of man and woman in marriage. At a wedding, the crowd gathers to sing "Alleluia" and to affirm the goodness of this marriage. The Church teaches us that the whole assembly together actively gives praise and thanks to God during any liturgical celebration. This pertains in a particular way to a wedding, where two families come together and friends from various corners of your lives are asked to witness (give assent to) your marriage.

There are many ways for couples to emphasize the important role of the assembly in their wedding ceremony: family and friends might be invited to sit together without concern for a "bride's side" and a "groom's side"; greeters can provide guests with a simple printed program or worship aid containing the order of the service, readings, and hymns, encouraging everyone to participate; and trained lectors and eucharistic ministers might be recruited from among your family members and friends.

There is cultural pressure to make your wedding day as a day when everything is perfect, and it is absolutely appropriate to dress up and make things beautiful to celebrate your love for each other. It is also good to ponder how you can celebrate your marriage as the beginning of a new community of disciples devoted to doing your part in bringing God's reign of justice a little closer. For example, out of concern for social justice, some couples are choosing minimal expenditure on clothing, decorations, and the reception and taking a collection for the poor during the liturgy. Like the wedding in this reading from Revelation, your wedding can be a celebration of love within a community that rejoices in God's triumph and hopes for a better world.

Alleluia Verses and Verses before the Gospel

E1
(OCM 56)
> R. Alleluia, alleluia.
> **May the** Lord **bless you from Zion,**
> **He who made both heaven and earth.** R.

Or, during Lent:
E2
1John 4:8b and 11
> R. (Psalm 81:2) Sing joyfully to God our strength.
> **God is love.**
> **Let us love one another, as God has loved us.** R.

E3
1 John 4:7b
(804–1)
> R. Alleluia, alleluia.
> **Everyone who loves is begotten of God and knows God.** R.

E4
1 John 4:8b and 11
(804–2)
> R. Alleluia, alleluia.
> **God is love.**
> **Let us love one another, as God has loved us.** R.

E5
1 John 4:12
(804–3)
> R. Alleluia, alleluia.
> **If we love one another,**
> **God remains in us**
> **and his love is brought to perfection in us.** R.

E6
1 John 4:16
(804–4)
> R. Alleluia, alleluia.
> **Whoever remains in love,**
> **remains in God and God in him.** R.

Gospel Readings

F1

Matthew 5:1–12a
(805–1)

Rejoice and be glad, for your
reward will be great in heaven.

✠ **A reading from the holy Gospel according to Matthew**

When Jesus saw the crowds, he went up the mountain,
    and after he had sat down, his disciples came to him.
He began to teach them, saying:

> "Blessed are the poor in spirit,
>> for theirs is the Kingdom of heaven.
>
> Blessed are they who mourn,
>> for they will be comforted.
>
> Blessed are the meek,
>> for they will inherit the land.
>
> Blessed are they who hunger and thirst for righteousness,
>> for they will be satisfied.
>
> Blessed are the merciful,
>> for they will be shown mercy.
>
> Blessed are the clean of heart,
>> for they will see God.
>
> Blessed are the peacemakers,
>> for they will be called children of God.
>
> Blessed are they who are persecuted for the sake of righteousness,
>> for theirs is the Kingdom of heaven.
>
> Blessed are you when they insult you and persecute you
>> and utter every kind of evil against you falsely because of me.
>
> Rejoice and be glad,
>> for your reward will be great in heaven."

The Gospel of the Lord.

The Word Brought Home

Some of you will recognize this reading as the Beatitudes, the first part of the famous Sermon on the Mount from Matthew's gospel. In this passage, Jesus describes for his listeners what their lives will be like if they decide to follow him. Jesus challenges them and us to accept a deeper code of life than even the Ten Commandments and the Law. This is a code of life that will make us "blessed," Jesus says, using a word that can also be translated as "happy." In this reading, Jesus calls his followers to a new way of thinking and acting and helps us see that who we are and what our stance towards life is are what make us blessed or happy—not what we have, or even what we do, but the manner in which we live.

What makes you happy—truly happy? Does your future spouse make you happy? Does your job, your possessions, or your hobbies make you happy? Are you happy by nature or because you were raised in a happy or blessed home? A mature Christian knows that the Beatitudes encourage a way of life that takes a lifetime to fully appreciate. Though the happiness that accompanies this way of life often seems elusive, it is well worth seeking. We are reminded by this reading that being merciful, seeking justice, being peacemakers, mourning losses with others, and remaining faithful will bring us happiness and eventual reward in heaven. The Beatitudes are demanding. They are radically counterculture to how many suggest we live and are a way of life to be embraced.

The wisdom of many mature, happily married couples will tell you that you can't change your partner after marriage even if you think so beforehand. Both of you will change; life will change you as it throws a lot of things—good and bad—your way. You will also change each other as you learn how to be married, but you cannot control or force most of what will change. The Church calls you to face all these things together as a married couple—loving, supporting, and challenging each other through thick and thin. The Beatitudes provide you with a wonderful code of interaction for your marriage. Allow this code to shape the way you treat each other as well as the way you live together within your wider community and the world. Live the Beatitudes, and you will know happiness; indeed, you will be blessed.

F2

Matthew 5:13–16
(805–2)

You are the light of the world.

✠ **A reading from the holy Gospel according to Matthew**

Jesus said to his disciples:
"You are the salt of the earth.
But if salt loses its taste, with what can it be seasoned?
It is no longer good for anything
    but to be thrown out and trampled underfoot.
You are the light of the world.
A city set on a mountain cannot be hidden.
Nor do they light a lamp and then put it under a bushel basket;
    it is set on a lamp stand,
      where it gives light to all in the house.
Just so, your light must shine before others,
    that they may see your good deeds
    and glorify your heavenly Father."

The Gospel of the Lord.

The Word Brought Home

In this passage from the Gospel of Matthew, Jesus calls his disciples to be salt of the earth and light of the world, but what does that mean? How exactly are Christians supposed to light up the world and bring it flavor? From the placement of this exhortation between the Beatitudes (see the previous reading) and the instruction on the Law—including commands about loving our enemies, giving alms, and not making the pursuit of wealth the center of our life—the author tells us that those who follow Christ are supposed to be models for others.

Christians are called in the gospels to a distinctive way of life. To the extent that married couples live this out, they are a sacrament or symbol of God's love for each other, for their children, and for everyone around them. In and through their marriage, they experience and allow others to experience God's love.

The Catholic vision of marriage is radical in its insistence that, to be a sacrament, a couple must be and live both for themselves and for others. The concept of living for others is crucial, but to be for others, a couple first has to be for themselves. We call marriage a sacrament of human friendship and insist that it is through our most intimate relationships that we taste something of divine love. In *On the Family* (a teaching document explaining the role of the Christian family in today's world), St. John Paul II calls spouses to accept the "gift of the sacrament of matrimony" by attending to the "task" of loving each other. In contrast to those who advocate a simplistic focus on the family, he describes home as the place where we can fulfill our deepest longings to love and be loved. John Paul II calls for a commitment to

"forming a community of persons." He calls spouses not just to stay married but also to grow deeper in love.

Christian marriage, then, is more than belonging to another; this is what gives our vision a depth lacking in most other understandings of marriage. For John Paul II, the self-giving of spouses to each other is the foundation of the family but not its only end. This love is meant to spill over as couples raise their children, live simply, welcome others into their home, and strive to transform the world around them through works of charity and justice.

This is a vision of a family living for itself and for others, of a loving couple committed to each other, their children, and the common good. Grounded in the belonging of the home but not limited by it, we can embrace the solidarity of being for others and live marriage as the adventure God intended it to be. In our own unique way, we can be salt of the earth and light for the world.

F3   A wise man built his house on rock.

Matthew 7:21, 24–29 or 7:21, 24–25
(805–3)
For the short form, omit bracketed text.

☦ **A reading from the holy Gospel according to Matthew**

Jesus said to his disciples:
"Not everyone who says to me, 'Lord, Lord,'
    will enter the Kingdom of heaven,
    but only the one who does the will of my Father in heaven.

"Everyone who listens to these words of mine and acts on them
    will be like a wise man who built his house on rock.
The rain fell, the floods came,
    and the winds blew and buffeted the house.
But it did not collapse; it had been set solidly on rock.

[And everyone who listens to these words of mine
    but does not act on them
    will be like a fool who built his house on sand.
The rain fell, the floods came,
    and the winds blew and buffeted the house.
And it collapsed and was completely ruined."

When Jesus finished these words,
    the crowds were astonished at his teaching,
    for he taught them as one having authority,
    and not as their scribes.]

The Gospel of the Lord.

The Word Brought Home

Have you ever driven through a torrential downpour? It is pretty scary stuff. What a contrast it presents to that beautiful spring day when the flowers were in full bloom and the love of your life was telling you how much he or she treasured you. We have all seen the pictures from natural disasters—earthquakes, floods, wildfires, and the horror of homes destroyed. These pictures contrast greatly with the secure home in which you likely imagine owning and raising a family. These images of the destructive force of nature remind us of the preciousness of life and the short time we have together, but they also remind us of the importance of building a firm foundation. In this passage from Matthew's gospel, Jesus uses the metaphor of building a house to teach about building a strong spiritual life; he is quite clear about how to "build a house" that will last and help us to weather the storms of life.

Your engagement is a time of great joy. There are many tasks that have to be done as you prepare for the big day. As beautiful and perfect as that wedding day you are planning at this time will be, the foundation for a lifetime of marriage needs to be established at this time as well.

Like many engaged couples, the two of you may have already weathered significant storms together. These may be storms between the two of you or storms in which you have been caught up because of relationships with family and friends. Perhaps you have waited anxiously for your fiancé to return from military deployment or recover from a critical or extended illness, or you may have helped your fiancé through a hard loss such as a family member's death or the loss of a good job. You have likely weathered the storms of disagreements, hurt feelings, and misunderstandings both large and small. You know by now how the building blocks of your relationship have been and will continue to be tested.

God's will for your marriage is that you build a strong foundation. Learn to deal with conflict in healthy ways: listen to each other, talk things through, show affection, laugh together, and do not let small issues become bigger than they need to be. Learn to support each other in good times and bad and challenge each other to continual growth in mind, body, and soul. Learn to be patient and compassionate toward your spouse even when you don't really want to. Build the house of your marriage on rock—a firm foundation of love, faithful companionship, and enduring commitment.

F4*   What God has united, man must not separate.
Matthew 19:3–6
(805-4)

✝ A reading from the holy Gospel according to Matthew

Some Pharisees approached Jesus, and tested him, saying,
  "Is it lawful for a man to divorce his wife for any cause whatever?"
He said in reply, "Have you not read that from the beginning
  the Creator made them male and female and said,
  For this reason a man shall leave his father and mother
  and be joined to his wife, and the two shall become one flesh?
So they are no longer two, but one flesh.
Therefore, what God has joined together, man must not separate."

The Gospel of the Lord.

The Word Brought Home

When asked about the moral legitimacy of divorce, Jesus replies with a statement about marriage, pointing back to Genesis and giving us a beautiful image of a man and woman clinging to each other. The term "one flesh" would have suggested to Jesus' listeners a union that was sexual, familial, personal, and spiritual. Because they are so close, these persons cannot be broken apart. Separation becomes unthinkable, even impossible.

But how does any one couple become one body, one flesh? Just as one can only become a better musician or athlete by practicing, so, too, a couple becomes "more married" by engaging in shared practices that bring them closer together. Many aspects of modern culture suggest that some couples just get lucky, but most of us know that love is a matter of the will, of deciding every day to love, and of engaging in practices that build unity.

St. John Paul II described sex as "total self-giving." A couple seeking to become one flesh should be committed to an ongoing sexual practice in which they strive to give their very selves to each other. This requires vulnerability, sacrifice, and pleasure. We say, in effect, "I'm not going to any other place or to anyone else. I'll pour all my relational energy into you." Committed in this way, spouses are free to be increasingly vulnerable with each other over time and to come forward with their desires to experience pleasure.

Good sexual practice involves self-sacrifice. True self-giving love can only come about through the pursuit of pleasure. If both spouses do not desire pleasure for themselves, they are not fully loving themselves or connecting with their partner. On the other hand, the spouse who does not seek the pleasure of their partner fails to embrace a necessary measure of sacrifice that love requires. Binding oneself to a changing spouse over time and committing to staying passionately engaged may sometimes require sacrifice. At times, retreating into oneself would be the easier way, but self-gift is not always easy, and neither is self-giving sex.

Though a couple shares many bodily experiences, sex is unique to marital friendship and plays a key role in the development of one-flesh unity. If a couple is faithfully committed to remaining connected, they will seek to maintain the sexual side of their life together. Honoring and nurturing sexual desire will nurture bodily belonging and increase their self-giving.

What does pleasure have to do with self-giving sex? Everything. If we lose sight of this reality, we will spiritualize sex out of recognition. Sex is what God gave human beings. Our very physical drives suggest our neediness, dependence, and the fact that we were created for connection. They point us squarely toward each other until we rest in each other's arms, fully intertwined.

The couple who refuses to let their sexual practice die even during the most challenging times of their marriage places their commitment to one-flesh union at the center of their lives. They are saying to each other over and over, "I love you. I still want to be with you. I will always want to be with you." And that is good.

F5

This is the greatest and the first commandment.
The second is like it.

Matthew 22:35–40
(805–5)

✠ A reading from the holy Gospel according to Matthew

One of the Pharisees, a scholar of the law, tested Jesus by asking,
 "Teacher, which commandment in the law is the greatest?"
He said to him,
 "You shall love the Lord, your God,
 with all your heart,
 with all your soul,
 and with all your mind.
This is the greatest and the first commandment.
The second is like it:
 You shall love your neighbor as yourself.
The whole law and the prophets depend on these two commandments."

The Gospel of the Lord.

F6*

They are no longer two, but one flesh.

Mark 10:6–9
(805–6)

✠ A reading from the holy Gospel according to Mark

Jesus said:
"From the beginning of creation,
 God made them male and female.
For this reason a man shall leave his father and mother
 and be joined to his wife,
 and the two shall become one flesh.
So they are no longer two but one flesh.
Therefore what God has joined together,
 no human being must separate."

The Gospel of the Lord.

The Word Brought Home

We all entertain notions of what kind of person a friend or loved one should be. You also know what type of individual you want your future spouse to be. But when we truly love, we pass beyond both of these and accept the loved one simply as she or he is. We know the person well: the faults and virtues, the ups and downs, the positive points and the negative characteristics. I may not care for this or that aspect of your personality, and I wish you would change here or improve there. Nevertheless, and more significantly, I take you as you stand before me; I love you just as you are.

That all sounds very poetic, yet in everyday married life, such acceptance may not come easily. Acceptance demands effort and so does the adjustment that necessarily flows from it. You may notice with surprise after a few months of married life that you are quite irritated by many of your new spouse's habits. At first those differences may be accepted as an unchangeable part of each person's temperament. But later the practical ramifications of those traits may call for further changes.

If your spouse likes to sleep in, will you feel resentment over changing the baby's diaper at 6:30 a.m., getting the kids' breakfast together alone, and leaving for work without a farewell kiss? If you like to get to bed early, will your spouse feel annoyed that you never seem able to stay awake long enough to watch a late-night movie or talk seriously after the children are in bed or that you don't like to linger in bed in the morning? To accept and adjust to differing habits takes some giving.

Such an accepting-adjusting pattern of life begins well before the wedding day and will last as long as the marriage does. You will know which areas of living together are most taxing for you as individuals, as a couple, and later as a larger family unit if you are blessed with children. So be ready for those concerns and use your best interpersonal skills when problems arise, remembering always that God is love and, in some mysterious way, has drawn you together in that same love.

But God leaves you free to make that love grow or allow it to slip backward, to keep it alive or let it wither and die. The Lord will help you forge a fantastic future, if you do your share. Joy in marriage much beyond your expectations and happiness far exceeding that which you now experience lie ahead. The only requirement is your willingness to love, to give, to accept, and to adjust. This will at times seem like a huge condition to meet, but keep in mind the community of friends and family who will witness your vows and the support of the Church who calls you into and supports you in this holy union called marriage.

F7*

John 2:1–11
(805–7)

Jesus did this as the beginning
of his signs in Cana in Galilee.

✠ A reading from the holy Gospel according to John

> There was a wedding in Cana in Galilee,
>> and the mother of Jesus was there.
> Jesus and his disciples were also invited to the wedding.
> When the wine ran short,
>> the mother of Jesus said to him,
>> "They have no wine."
> And Jesus said to her,
>> "Woman, how does your concern affect me?
> My hour has not yet come."
> His mother said to the servers,
>> "Do whatever he tells you."
> Now there were six stone water jars there for Jewish ceremonial
>> washings,
>> each holding twenty to thirty gallons.
> Jesus told them,
>> "Fill the jars with water."
> So they filled them to the brim.
> Then he told them,
>> "Draw some out now and take it to the headwaiter."
> So they took it.
> And when the headwaiter tasted the water that had become wine,
>> without knowing where it came from
>> (although the servants who had drawn the water knew),
>> the headwaiter called the bridegroom and said to him,
>> "Everyone serves good wine first,
>> and then when people have drunk freely, an inferior one;
>> but you have kept the good wine until now."
> Jesus did this as the beginning of his signs in Cana in Galilee
>> and so revealed his glory,
>> and his disciples began to believe in him.

The Gospel of the Lord.

The Word Brought Home

The Gospel of John, from which this reading comes, begins with a dramatic prologue: "In the beginning was the Word, and the Word was with God, and the Word was God." The language explicitly recalls the opening lines of the creation story in Genesis and walks us through six days that describe the testimony of John the Baptist about Jesus. On the seventh day, the day in Genesis on which God rested after the first creation, Jesus performs this miracle of changing water into wine at a wedding feast. The wedding has symbolic importance as it is where Jesus takes on his public role as the Word made flesh. Mary, his mother, decides how this will take place. The story tells us that Mary sympathizes with the new couple; she wants them to prolong the joy of their wedding day by serving wine to their beloved friends and family. Jesus, perhaps reluctant because he is unsure that this is the right occasion to begin his public ministry, gives in. Perhaps it is because he simply trusts his mother; perhaps she helps him see that any opportunity to show the generous love of God is the right occasion.

It is good to imagine Jesus present at our own weddings, blessing and extending the joy of the guests. There is something beautiful about the idea that Christ wants only to be part of this moment of great joy: to use it for no other end than celebration itself. It is no surprise that the kingdom of God is elsewhere likened to a wedding banquet (as in Matthew 22), since it is an image of feasting and rejoicing. Similarly, the book of Revelation describes the end of time as a wedding banquet where "there shall be no more death or mourning." It is comforting to imagine the wedding being the beginning of a time of great joy. Life will present challenges, to be sure, but the promise of the Gospel is that Jesus is present with us, extending our joy even in the face of challenges.

In his masterful novel *The Brothers Karamazov*, Fyodor Dostoevsky describes a young novice monk, Alyosha, who hears the story of the Wedding at Cana at prayer over the body of his deceased mentor, Father Zossima. Alyosha is moved by how hopeful the story is and how joyful the couple at the wedding must have been because of the generosity Jesus shows in his first miracle. He meditates on this generosity: "He is changing the water into wine that the gladness of the guests may not be cut short." God's own joy for his beloved children motivates Alyosha to depart from the monastery and sojourn in the secular world. May the joy and hope of your wedding day also draw you into the world, to share the love you've found with all you meet.

F8   Remain in my love.
John 15:9–12
(805-8)

✠ A reading from the holy Gospel according to John

Jesus said to his disciples:
"As the Father loves me, so I also love you.
Remain in my love.
If you keep my commandments, you will remain in my love,
        just as I have kept my Father's commandments
        and remain in his love.

"I have told you this so that my joy might be in you
        and your joy might be complete.
This is my commandment: love one another as I love you."

The Gospel of the Lord.

F9   This is my commandment: love one another.
John 15:12–16
(805-9)

✠ A reading from the holy Gospel according to John

Jesus said to his disciples:
"This is my commandment: love one another as I love you.
No one has greater love than this,
        to lay down one's life for one's friends.
You are my friends if you do what I command you.
I no longer call you slaves,
        because a slave does not know what his master is doing.
I have called you friends,
        because I have told you everything I have heard from my Father.
It was not you who chose me, but I who chose you
        and appointed you to go and bear fruit that will remain,
        so that whatever you ask the Father in my name he may give you."

The Gospel of the Lord.

The Word Brought Home

The early days of a romance are quite fun. It all seems too good to be true. How could I be so lucky? Is this the one?

With time, however, we start to discover quirks and flaws in our new love; then the small, irritating habits; and finally those things that drive us absolutely nuts. At that point the relationship either ends or we begin to learn how to live with each other despite the challenges of doing so. In short, we learn how to "remain."

These readings from the Gospel of John were spoken during the final meal Jesus shared with his closest disciples on the night before he died. These disciples had been with Jesus throughout his ministry. They had eaten with him, prayed with him, journeyed with him, and listened to him. When his words became too challenging for others, they stuck by him. These were no longer just followers but friends. And his last request of them was to remain.

Remaining in a relationship is not an easy thing to do, and our culture does little to teach the skills needed for long-term relationships. Our news media, entertainment, and political structures thrive on controversy and debate, sound bites, and critiques. Legal advice warns us against admitting fault or asking forgiveness. Athletic competitions spark a win-at-all-costs mentality. The patterns of speech, interaction, and communication common in so much of our culture are detrimental when used in marriage and family life. Many of us grow up desiring lifelong relationships, but we discover that we are missing the skills needed to sustain them. When times get tough, do we have what it takes to remain?

Remaining in marriage requires the ability to share physical space even as you wish that your spouse would pick up her clothes from the bathroom floor or put his dishes directly into the dishwasher. Moreover, remaining requires sharing emotional space even when it is tempting to withdraw. It implies the courage to listen even when you hear things you don't want to hear and to keep trying to communicate even when you feel you aren't being heard. It demands continuing the conversation even when it doesn't seem to be reaching any amenable conclusion.

There are times in marriage when a couple feels at an absolute impasse, powerless to see a way forward, with neither partner able to further compromise. These can be gray, foggy, uncomfortable places. No one wants to set up lodging there. And yet sometimes we are called to simply remain in these places, waiting until one partner unexpectedly is moved to make a shift or—more often—a previously unseen option surfaces.

Many voices tell us that, when we are unhappy, unfulfilled, disillusioned, or simply bored in a relationship, it is time to move on. Yet Jesus tells us that it is in remaining that we, too, can discover the mysterious truth he wants to share with us: that our own joy "might be complete."

F10   That they may be brought to perfection as one.

John 17:20–26 or 17:20–23
(805–10)
For the short form, omit bracketed text.

✠ **A reading from the holy Gospel according to John**

Jesus raised his eyes to heaven and said:
"I pray not only for my disciples,
    but also for those who will believe in me through their word,
    so that they may all be one,
    as you, Father, are in me and I in you,
    that they also may be in us,
    that the world may believe that you sent me.
And I have given them the glory you gave me,
    so that they may be one, as we are one,
    I in them and you in me,
    that they may be brought to perfection as one,
    that the world may know that you sent me,
    and that you loved them even as you loved me.

[Father, they are your gift to me.
I wish that where I am they also may be with me,
    that they may see my glory that you gave me,
    because you loved me before the foundation of the world.
Righteous Father, the world also does not know you,
    but I know you, and they know that you sent me.
I made known to them your name and I will make it known,
    that the love with which you loved me
    may be in them and I in them."]

The Gospel of the Lord.

The Word Brought Home

We live in a diverse world that is rife with conflict. Daily headlines bear witness to ways in which the differences that exist among us—man or woman, brown, white or black, liberal or conservative, and native born or immigrant—have contributed to anger, violence, and war. In our friendships and social media networking, we often find ourselves retreating to safe, homogenous spaces where we can hang out with people like us, who think similar thoughts and share our point of view.

Every marriage is a daring step out of that safe space and into the fray. Marriage binds a man and a woman and asks them to live with each other for the rest of their lives, bridging the gender divide along with many others. Often, it binds persons of different economic classes, different political leanings, and different cultural heritages. Even people who seem to be two peas in a pod may quickly discover they have markedly dissimilar personalities and preferences. Living in close contact seems to accentuate differences not evident before.

In contrast to the nightly news, Christian marriage bears witness that differences don't have to divide—they can unite, enrich, and strengthen. As early as the fifth century, St. Augustine argued that marriage beyond family lines served to widen the sense of community and distribute the riches of Christianity toward a more just society. This argument only affirmed what the Church had long been practicing in its discouragement of marriage between family members even when it was common practice within the wider culture. Love makes possible what peace treaties and trade agreements in the world cannot. It draws and binds together people of diverse backgrounds—with strikingly different needs, desires, and patterns of living—into thriving family units.

In this passage from the Gospel of John, Jesus prays that his disciples can know the kind of oneness with each other he shares with his Father. He says their unity will witness that what he has preached is true. Their oneness will be a sign that the reign of God is possible and has already begun. They will give hope to the world.

Consider the differences that lie between the two of you, and consider the ways that your love has bridged those differences and enriched your life. Have you ever thought about how your capacity to do this is a sign of hope for the world? It is a lot of weight to carry, and yet it is precisely what the Church believes marriage is and does. When the community is discouraged about violence and division in the world; when it grieves the effects of poverty, homelessness, and inadequate health care; and when it is anxious about harmony within its own ranks, it can look to you and to all married couples who are living faithfully and remember that what Jesus said remains true—oneness, unity, is possible.

The Celebration of Matrimony

The heart of a Catholic wedding is the exchange of vows, formally called "The Consent" because by them you say yes to the love God has given you and to the married life.

On pages 88–95, you will find that each bold letter-numeral code is paired with a tag that reads Form 1 (Within Mass), Form 2 (Without Mass), or Form 3 (Between a Catholic and a Catechumen or a Non-Christian). These correspond to the three forms of the Celebration of Matrimony that are outlined on page 10 and will be used by parish staff to prepare the liturgical books for your wedding. **Be sure to keep in mind which form of the celebration will be used at your wedding (see page 2) and then follow that form through the various choices you are asked to make.**

The Questions before the Consent

The presider will invite you and your witnesses forward, then pray:

G1 (Form 1)
G2 (Form 2)

> Dearly beloved,
> you have come together into the house of the Church,
> so that in the presence of the Church's minister and the
>   community
> your intention to enter into Marriage
> may be strengthened by the Lord with a sacred seal.
> Christ abundantly blesses the love that binds you.
> Through a special Sacrament,
> he enriches and strengthens
> those he has already consecrated by Holy Baptism,
> that they may be faithful to each other for ever
> and assume all the responsibilities of married life.
> And so, in the presence of the Church,
> I ask you to state your intentions.

The priest or deacon will then ask about your readiness to marry.

> N. and N., have you come here to enter into Marriage
> without coercion, freely and wholeheartedly?

The bridegroom and the bride each say:
I have.

The priest or deacon continues:
Are you prepared, as you follow the path of Marriage,
to love and honor each other for as long as you both shall live?

The bridegroom and the bride each say:
I am.

The following question may be omitted if, for example, the couple is advanced in years.
Are you prepared to accept children lovingly from God and bring
them up according to the law of Christ and his Church?

The bridegroom and the bride each say:
I am.

G3 (Form 3)

Dearly beloved,
you have come together here
before a minister of the Church
and in the presence of the community
so that your intention to enter into Marriage
may be strengthened by the Lord with a sacred seal,
and your love be enriched with his blessing,
so that you may have strength
to be faithful to each other for ever
and to assume all the responsibilities of married life.
And so, in the presence of the Church,
I ask you to state your intentions.

The priest or deacon will then ask about your readiness to marry.
N. and N., have you come here to enter into Marriage
without coercion, freely and wholeheartedly?

The bridegroom and the bride each say:
I have.

The priest or deacon who presides continues:
Are you prepared, as you follow the path of Marriage,
to love and honor each other for as long as you both shall live?

The bridegroom and the bride each say:
I am.

The following question may be omitted if, for example, the couple is advanced in years.

**Are you prepared to accept children lovingly from God
and to bring them up
according to the law of Christ and his Church?**

The bridegroom and the bride each say:
I am.

The Consent (Marriage Vows)

Next are your marriage vows. The Church calls this "The Consent" because you are consenting to God's call to Christian marriage. You are saying "I do" to the love he has planted in your hearts and to becoming a visible sign of his love in the world. By exchanging marriage vows—by giving your consent—you say yes.

Please choose from the First or Second formula for the vows and whether you want to say the words yourself or simply say "I do" after the minister poses the vows as questions. Talk with the priest or deacon about how to handle the exchange of vows. You can recite them from memory, read them from a card, or be prompted by the priest or deacon.

Please be sure to record your choice on the selection form.

First Formula

H1 (Form 1)
H5 (Form 2)
H9 (Form 3)

Since it is your intention to enter the covenant of Holy Matrimony, join your right hands and declare your consent before God and his Church.

You will join hands and the groom begins:
I, N., take you, N., to be my wife.
I promise to be faithful to you,

in good times and in bad,
in sickness and in health,
to love you and to honor you all the days of my life.

The bride says:
I, N., take you, N., to be my husband.
I promise to be faithful to you,
in good times and in bad,
in sickness and in health,
to love you and to honor you all the days of my life.

H3 (Form 1)
H7 (Form 2)
H11 (Form 3)

If, however, it seems preferable for pastoral reasons, the presider may obtain consent from the couple through questions.

First he asks the bridegroom:
N., do you take N. to be your wife?
Do you promise to be faithful to her
in good times and in bad,
in sickness and in health,
to love her and to honor her all the days of your life?
The groom: I do.

Then he asks the bride:
N., do you take N. to be your husband?
Do you promise to be faithful to him
in good times and in bad,
in sickness and in health,
to love him and to honor him all the days of your life?
The bride: I do.

Second Formula

H2 (Form 1)
H6 (Form 2)
H10 (Form 3)

The groom says:
I, N., take you N., for my lawful wife,
to have and to hold, from this day forward,
for better, for worse,

for richer, for poorer,
in sickness and in health,
to love and to cherish
until death do us part.

The bride says:
I, N., take you, N., for my lawful husband,
to have and to hold, from this day forward,
for better, for worse,
for richer, for poorer,
in sickness and in health,
to love and to cherish
until death do us part.

H4 (Form 1)
H8 (Form 2)
H12 (Form 3)
The presider may obtain consent from the couple through questions.

First the one presiding asks the groom:
N., **do you take N. for your lawful wife,**
To have and to hold, from this day forward,
for better, for worse,
for richer, for poorer,
in sickness and in health,
to love and to cherish
until death do you part?
The groom: **I do.**

Next, the one presiding asks the bride:
N., **do you take N. for your lawful husband,**
to have and to hold, from this day forward,
for better, for worse,
for richer, for poorer,
in sickness and in health,
to love and to cherish
until death do you part?
The bride: **I do.**

Reception of the Consent

On behalf of the Church and the people of God, the priest or deacon receives the consent of the couple using one of two formulas, by saying:

H13 (Form 1)
H14 (Form 2)
H15 (Form 3)

(a) **May the Lord in his kindness strengthen the consent**
   you have declared before the Church,
   and graciously bring to fulfillment his blessing within you.
   What God joins together, let no one put asunder.

The priest or deacon invites those present to praise God:
Let us bless the Lord.

All reply:
Thanks be to God.

Another acclamation may be sung or said.

or:

(b) **May the God of Abraham, the God of Isaac, the God of Jacob,**
   the God who joined together our first parents in paradise,
   strengthen and bless in Christ
   the consent you have declared before the Church,
   so that what God joins together, no one may put asunder.

The priest or deacon invites those present to praise God:
Let us bless the Lord.

All reply:
Thanks be to God.

Another acclamation may be sung or said.

Blessing and Giving of Rings

Your wedding rings are a symbol of the vows you take. The circles convey the unending nature of your bond, and the precious metal expresses its strength and immeasurable value.

Choose a blessing for your rings and record it on your selection form.

94   Together for Life

I1 (Form 1)
I2 (Form 2)
I3 (Form 3)

> May the Lord bless ✞ these rings
> which you will give to each other
> as a sign of love and fidelity.
>
> All respond: **Amen.**

I4 (Form 1, 2, or 3)

> Bless, O Lord, these rings,
> which we bless ✞ in your name,
> so that those who wear them
> may remain entirely faithful to each other,
> abide in peace and in your will,
> and live always in mutual charity.
> Through Christ our Lord.
>
> All respond: **Amen.**

I5 (Form 1, 2, or 3)

> Bless ✞ and sanctify your servants
> in their love, O Lord,
> and let these rings, a sign of their faithfulness,
> remind them of their love for one another.
> Through Christ our Lord.
>
> All respond: **Amen.**

As the bridegroom places his wife's ring on her ring finger, he may say:
N., **receive this ring as a sign of my love and fidelity.**
In the name of the Father, and of the Son, and of the Holy Spirit.

As the bride places her husband's ring on his ring finger, she may say:
N., **receive this ring as a sign of my love and fidelity.**
In the name of the Father, and of the Son, and of the Holy Spirit.

If bride or groom is not Christian, omit the Sign of the Cross.

Blessing and Giving of the *Arras* (Optional)
I6 (Form 1)
I7 (Form 2)
I8 (Form 3)
If you wish to include this blessing (see page 8), please indicate this on your selection sheet.

> The one presiding says:
> **Bless, ✝ O Lord, these *arras***
> **that N. and N. will give to each other**
> **and pour over them the abundance of your good gifts.**
>
> The husband takes the *arras* and hands them over to his wife, saying:
> **N., receive these *arras* as a pledge of God's blessing**
> **and a sign of the good gifts we will share.**
>
> The wife takes the *arras* and hands them over to the husband, saying:
> **N., receive these *arras* as a pledge of God's blessing**
> **and a sign of the good gifts we will share.**

Universal Prayer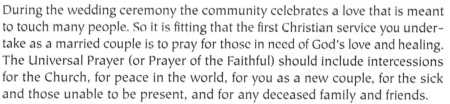

During the wedding ceremony the community celebrates a love that is meant to touch many people. So it is fitting that the first Christian service you undertake as a married couple is to pray for those in need of God's love and healing. The Universal Prayer (or Prayer of the Faithful) should include intercessions for the Church, for peace in the world, for you as a new couple, for the sick and those unable to be present, and for any deceased family and friends.

You can choose one of the sample sets of intercessions that follow or write your own if the parish in which you celebrate your wedding so allows. These sample prayers are available in electronic form at TogetherforLifeOnline.com. If you are invited to write your own, visit the same website for instructions and a simple worksheet that will help you do so.

J1

> The priest or deacon begins:
> **Dear brothers and sisters,**
> **as we call to mind the special gift of grace and charity**
> **by which God has been pleased to crown and consecrate**
> **the love of our sister N. and our brother N.,**
> **let us commend them to the Lord.**

A reader continues:
That these faithful Christians, N. and N.,
newly joined in Holy Matrimony,
may always enjoy health and well-being,
let us pray to the Lord.

R. Lord, we ask you, hear our prayer

Or another appropriate response of the people.

That he will bless their covenant
as he chose to sanctify marriage at Cana in Galilee,
let us pray to the Lord. R.

That they be granted perfect and fruitful love,
peace and strength,
and that they bear faithful witness to the name of Christian,
let us pray to the Lord. R.

That the Christian people
may grow in virtue day by day
and that all who are burdened by any need
may receive the help of grace from above,
let us pray to the Lord. R.

That the grace of the Sacrament
will be renewed by the Holy Spirit
in all married persons here present,
let us pray to the Lord. R.

The priest or deacon concludes:
Graciously pour out upon this husband and wife, O Lord,
the Spirit of your love,
to make them one heart and one soul,
so that nothing whatever may divide those you have joined
and no harm come to those you have filled with your blessing.
Through Christ our Lord.

R. Amen.

J2

The priest or deacon begins:
Dear brothers and sisters,
let us accompany this new family with our prayers,

that the mutual love of this couple may grow daily
and that God in his kindness
will sustain all families throughout the world.

A reader continues:
For this bride and groom,
and for their well-being as a family,
let us pray to the Lord.

R. Lord, we ask you, hear our prayer.

Or another appropriate response of the people.

For their relatives and friends,
and for all who have assisted this couple,
let us pray to the Lord. R.

For young people preparing to enter Marriage,
and for all whom the Lord is calling to another state in life,
let us pray to the Lord. R.

For all families throughout the world
and for lasting peace among all people,
let us pray to the Lord. R.

For all members of our families
who have passed from this world,
and for all the departed,
let us pray to the Lord. R.

For the Church, the holy People of God,
and for unity among all Christians,
let us pray to the Lord. R.

The priest or deacon concludes:
Lord Jesus, who are present in our midst,
as N. and N. seal their union
accept our prayer
and fill us with your Spirit.
Who live and reign for ever and ever.

R. Amen.

When using Form 2, Celebrating Matrimony without Mass, please turn to page 102.

The Liturgy of the Eucharist

(For Celebrating Matrimony within Mass)

The love that you share as husband and wife finds its source in the love God has for us. This love was made perfectly manifest in the suffering, death, and resurrection of Jesus whose sacrificial love freed us from sin and opened for us the gift of eternal life. In the Eucharist, his sacrifice of love is present again by the power of the Holy Spirit. Christ becomes for us the nourishment we need to love, forgive, and reach out to others in compassion. The bread and wine brought forth represent the gift of our lives to God, and in exchange God gives us the gift of his very self in the Eucharist.

Once the altar is prepared and the gifts brought forth, the priest will say one of the following prayers over the gifts, asking God to accept them along with the love offered by you as a couple.

Prayer over the Offerings

Choose one of these prayers and record it on your selection form.

K1

Receive, we pray, O Lord,
the offering made on the occasion
of this sealing of the sacred bond of Marriage,
and, just as your goodness is its origin,
may your providence guide its course.
Through Christ our Lord.

K2

Receive in your kindness, Lord,
the offerings we bring in gladness before you,
and in your fatherly love
watch over those you have joined in a sacramental covenant.
Through Christ our Lord.

K3

Show favor to our supplications, O Lord,
and receive with a kindly countenance
the oblations we offer for these your servants,
joined now in a holy covenant,
that through these mysteries
they may be strengthened
in love for one another and for you.
Through Christ our Lord.

Preface

The Eucharistic Prayer is then prayed by the priest in dialogue with the people. During the prayer the gifts of bread and wine, and we ourselves, become transformed into the Body and Blood of Christ. The Eucharistic Prayer begins with the Preface and moves through to the Great Amen.

Choose one of the following Prefaces and record it on your selection form.

L1   The dignity of the Marriage covenant

V. The Lord be with you.
R. And with your spirit.
V. Lift up your hearts.
R. We lift them up to the Lord.
V. Let us give thanks to the Lord our God.
R. It is right and just.

It is truly right and just, our duty and our salvation,
always and everywhere to give you thanks,
Lord, holy Father, almighty and eternal God.

For you have forged the covenant of Marriage
as a sweet yoke of harmony
and an unbreakable bond of peace,

so that the chaste and fruitful love of holy Matrimony
may serve to increase the children you adopt as your own.

By your providence and grace, O Lord,
you accomplish the wonder of this twofold design:
that, while the birth of children brings beauty to the world,
their rebirth in Baptism gives increase to the Church,
through Christ our Lord.

Through him, with the Angels and all the Saints,
we sing the hymn of your praise,
as without end we acclaim:

Holy, Holy, Holy Lord God of hosts.
Heaven and earth are full of your glory.
Hosanna in the highest.
Blessed is he who comes in the name of the Lord.
Hosanna in the highest.

L2   The great Sacrament of Matrimony

V. The Lord be with you.
R. And with your spirit.
V. Lift up your hearts.
R. We lift them up to the Lord.
V. Let us give thanks to the Lord our God.
R. It is right and just.

It is truly right and just, our duty and our salvation,
always and everywhere to give you thanks,
Lord, holy Father, almighty and eternal God,
through Christ our Lord.

For in him you have made a new covenant with your people,
so that, as you have redeemed man and woman
by the mystery of Christ's Death and Resurrection,
so in Christ you might make them partakers of divine nature
and joint heirs with him of heavenly glory.

In the union of husband and wife
you give a sign of Christ's loving gift of grace,
so that the Sacrament we celebrate
might draw us back more deeply
into the wondrous design of your love.

And so, with the Angels and all the Saints,
we praise you, and without end we acclaim:

Holy, Holy, Holy Lord God of hosts . . .

L3   Matrimony as a sign of divine love

V. The Lord be with you.
R. And with your spirit.
V. Lift up your hearts.
R. We lift them up to the Lord.
V. Let us give thanks to the Lord our God.
R. It is right and just.

It is truly right and just, our duty and our salvation,
always and everywhere to give you thanks,
Lord, holy Father, almighty and eternal God.

For you willed that the human race,
created by the gift of your goodness,
should be raised to such high dignity
that in the union of husband and wife
you might bestow a true image of your love.

For those you created out of charity
you call to the law of charity without ceasing
and grant them a share in your eternal charity.

And so, the Sacrament of holy Matrimony,
as the abiding sign of your own love,
consecrates the love of man and woman,
through Christ our Lord.

Through him, with the Angels and all the Saints,
we sing the hymn of your praise,
as without end we acclaim:

Holy, Holy, Holy Lord God of hosts . . .

Blessing and Placing of the *Lazo* or the Veil (Optional)

M (Form 1 or 2)

The rite of blessing and imposition of the *lazo* (wedding garland) or of the veil may take place before the Nuptial Blessing. The spouses remain kneeling in their place. If the *lazo* has not been placed earlier and it is now convenient to do so, it may be placed at this time; otherwise, a veil is placed over the head of the wife and the shoulders of the husband, thus symbolizing the bond that unites them (see page 8).

> The priest or deacon says:
> Bless, ✝ O Lord, this *lazo* (or, this veil),
> a symbol of the indissoluble union
> that N. and N. have established from this day forward
> before you and with your help.

The *lazo* (or the veil) is held by two family members or friends and is placed over the shoulders of the newly married couple.

The Nuptial Blessing

The Nuptial Blessing is the formal, extended blessing of the newly married couple. In it, the Church prays that the couple may continue to love each other, remain ever faithful to their marriage bond, be a sign of Christian discipleship and of God's enduring love to all those with whom they come in contact, and be good parents to any children with whom they are blessed.

This blessing offers everyone present a few moments to contemplate in prayer the wonderful commitment that you have made to each other, to God, and to all those gathered with you. Choose a Nuptial Blessing and record it on your selection form.

> For those using Form 3 of celebrating matrimony,
> M5 is used (page 111).
> NB: There is no M4 option provided here because M4 is a designation for texts used only by the priest or deacon presiding at your wedding and used in *The Order of Celebrating Matrimony Ritual Cards*.

M1

O God, who by your mighty power
created all things out of nothing,
and, when you had set in place
the beginnings of the universe,
formed man and woman in your own image,
making the woman an inseparable helpmate to the man,
that they might no longer be two, but one flesh,
and taught that what you were pleased to make one
must never be divided;

O God, who consecrated the bond of Marriage
by so great a mystery
that in the wedding covenant you foreshadowed
the Sacrament of Christ and his Church;

O God, by whom woman is joined to man
and the companionship they had in the beginning
is endowed with the one blessing
not forfeited by original sin
nor washed away by the flood.

Look now with favor on these your servants,
joined together in Marriage,
who ask to be strengthened by your blessing.
Send down on them the grace of the Holy Spirit
and pour your love into their hearts,
that they may remain faithful in the Marriage covenant.

May the grace of love and peace
abide in your daughter N.,
and let her always follow the example of those holy women
whose praises are sung in the Scriptures.

May her husband entrust his heart to her,
so that, acknowledging her as his equal
and his joint heir to the life of grace,
he may show her due honor
and cherish her always
with the love that Christ has for his Church.

And now, Lord, we implore you:
may these your servants
hold fast to the faith and keep your commandments;

made one in the flesh,
may they be blameless in all they do;
and with the strength that comes from the Gospel,
may they bear true witness to Christ before all;
(may they be blessed with children,
and prove themselves virtuous parents,
who live to see their children's children).

And grant that,
reaching at last together the fullness of years
for which they hope,
they may come to the life of the blessed
in the Kingdom of Heaven.
Through Christ our Lord.
R. Amen.

M2

Holy Father,
who formed man in your own image,
male and female you created them,
so that as husband and wife, united in body and heart,
they might fulfill their calling in the world;

O God, who, to reveal the great design you formed in your love,
willed that the love of spouses for each other
should foreshadow the covenant you graciously made with your
     people,
so that, by fulfillment of the sacramental sign,
the mystical marriage of Christ with his Church
might become manifest
in the union of husband and wife among your faithful;

Graciously stretch out your right hand
over these your servants (N. and N.), we pray,
and pour into their hearts the power of the Holy Spirit.

Grant, O Lord,
that, as they enter upon this sacramental union,
they may share with one another the gifts of your love
and, by being for each other a sign of your presence,
become one heart and one mind.

May they also sustain, O Lord, by their deeds
the home they are forming
(and prepare their children
to become members of your heavenly household
by raising them in the way of the Gospel).
Graciously crown with your blessings your daughter N.,
so that, by being a good wife (and mother),
she may bring warmth to her home with a love that is pure
and adorn it with welcoming graciousness.

Bestow a heavenly blessing also, O Lord,
on N., your servant,
that he may be a worthy, good and
faithful husband (and a provident father).

Grant, holy Father,
that, desiring to approach your table
as a couple joined in Marriage in your presence,
they may one day have the joy
of taking part in your great banquet in heaven.
Through Christ our Lord.
R. Amen.

M3

Holy Father, maker of the whole world,
who created man and woman in your own image
and willed that their union be crowned with your blessing,
we humbly beseech you for these your servants,
who are joined today in the Sacrament of Matrimony.

May your abundant blessing, Lord,
come down upon this bride, N.,
and upon N., her companion for life,
and may the power of your Holy Spirit
set their hearts aflame from on high,
so that, living out together the gift of Matrimony,
they may (adorn their family with children
and) enrich the Church.

In happiness may they praise you, O Lord,
in sorrow may they seek you out;
may they have the joy of your presence
to assist them in their toil,
and know that you are near
to comfort them in their need;
let them pray to you in the holy assembly
and bear witness to you in the world,
and after a happy old age,
together with the circle of friends that surrounds them,
may they come to the Kingdom of Heaven.
Through Christ our Lord.
R. Amen.

Although Communion is not commonly distributed when Form 2 (Matrimony without Mass) is celebrated, certain pastoral circumstances may suggest doing so. If Communion is to be distributed, the celebration concludes with the Lord's Prayer, Sign of Peace, Holy Communion, and then the Final Blessing.

If Communion is not to be distributed, the celebration concludes with a simple blessing followed by the Recessional. Turn to page 110 for information on the Recessional.

Sign of Peace

The exchange of a sign of peace during the liturgy allows the assembly to express their love and unity for each other before receiving Holy Communion.

Prayer after Communion

After the distribution of Communion is finished and the ministers have returned to their places, all will pray silently in thanksgiving. Then the priest will invite everyone to stand for one of the following prayers.

Make your choice from the following and record it on your selection form.

N1

By the power of this sacrifice, O Lord,
accompany with your loving favor
what in your providence you have instituted,
so as to make of one heart in love
those you have already joined in this holy union
(and replenished with the one Bread and the one Chalice).
Through Christ our Lord.

N2

Having been made partakers at your table,
we pray, O Lord,
that those who are united by the Sacrament of Marriage
may always hold fast to you
and proclaim your name to the world.
Through Christ our Lord.

N3

Grant, we pray, almighty God,
that the power of the Sacrament we have received
may find growth in these your servants
and that the effects of the sacrifice we have offered
may be felt by us all.
Through Christ our Lord.

The Conclusion of the Celebration

Final or Solemn Blessing
When Communion Is Distributed (Form 1) (Form 2)

The liturgy concludes with a solemn blessing, prayed over you by the priest or deacon. Each of the options for the final blessing is comprised of short prayers to which the assembly responds "Amen." At the end of the blessing the priest or deacon makes the sign of the cross over all those present. Please choose one of the following blessings and record it on your selection form.

O1

The priest, with hands extended over the bride and bridegroom, says:
May God the eternal Father
keep you of one heart in love for one another,
that the peace of Christ may dwell in you
and abide always in your home.
R. Amen.

May you be blessed in your children,
have solace in your friends
and enjoy true peace with everyone.
R. Amen.

May you be witnesses in the world to God's charity,
so that the afflicted and needy who have known your kindness
may one day receive you thankfully
into the eternal dwelling of God.
R. Amen.

And he blesses all present, adding:
**And may almighty God bless all of you, who are gathered here,
the Father, and the Son, ✝ and the Holy Spirit.**
R. Amen.

O2

The priest, with hands extended over the bride and bridegroom,
says:
**May God the all-powerful Father grant you his joy
and bless you in your children.**
R. Amen.

**May the Only Begotten Son of God
stand by you with compassion in good times and in bad.**
R. Amen.

**May the Holy Spirit of God
always pour forth his love into your hearts.**
R. Amen.

And he blesses all present, adding:
**And may almighty God bless all of you, who are gathered here,
the Father, and the Son, ✝ and the Holy Spirit.**
R. Amen.

O3

The priest, with hands extended over the bride and bridegroom,
says:
**May the Lord Jesus,
who graced the marriage at Cana by his presence,
bless you and your loved ones.**
R. Amen.

**May he, who loved the Church to the end,
unceasingly pour his love into your hearts.**
R. Amen.

**May the Lord grant
that, bearing witness to faith in his Resurrection,
you may await with joy the blessed hope to come.**
R. Amen.

And he blesses all present, adding:

And may almighty God bless all of you, who are gathered here, the Father, and the Son, ✝ and the Holy Spirit.
R. Amen.

Following the final blessing, the rite does not call for any specific dismissal. The presider will discuss with you what is appropriate and customary in your community.

Recessional

The recessional is meant to be a simple procession out of the church by the bride and groom and perhaps other members of the wedding party. The bride and groom generally process out first, followed by the two witnesses and then other members of the wedding party. The music chosen for this is often upbeat and spirited.

The Conclusion of the Celebration

(Form 3)

The Lord's Prayer

Following the Universal Prayer (J1, page 95, or J2, page 96), the one who presides continues:

> God the Father wills that his children be of one heart
> in charity;
> Let those who are Christian call upon him
> in the prayer of God's family,
> which our Lord Jesus Christ has taught us:

> And all the Christians continue:
> Our Father, who art in heaven . . .

Blessing and Placing of the *Lazo* or the Veil (Optional)
M

The rite of blessing and imposition of the *lazo* (wedding garland) or the veil may take place before the Nuptial Blessing. The spouses remain kneeling in their place. If the *lazo* has not been placed earlier and it is now convenient to do so, it may be placed at this time; otherwise, a veil is placed over the head of the wife and the shoulders of the husband, thus symbolizing the bond that unites them (see page 8).

> The priest or deacon says:
> Bless, ✣ O Lord, this *lazo* (or, this veil),
> a symbol of the indissoluble union
> that N. and N. have established from this day forward

before you and with your help.

The *lazo* (or the veil) is held by two family members or friends and is placed over the shoulders of the newly married couple.

Nuptial Blessing

As a rule, the Nuptial Blessing is said over the bride and bridegroom. Nevertheless, if circumstances suggest this, it may be omitted and, in this case, this prayer is said in place of the Nuptial Blessing.

> Be attentive to our prayers, O Lord,
> and in your kindness uphold
> what you have established
> for the increase of the human race,
> so that the union you have created
> may be kept safe by your assistance.
> Through Christ our Lord.
> R. Amen.

M5

When the Nuptial Blessing is prayed, this form of it is used:

> Holy Father, maker of the whole world,
> who created man and woman in your own image
> and willed that their union be crowned with your blessing,
> we humbly beseech you for these your servants,
> who are joined today in the Marriage covenant.
>
> May your abundant blessing, Lord,
> come down upon this bride, N.,
> and upon N., her companion for life,
> and may the power of your Holy Spirit
> set their hearts aflame from on high,
> so that, living out together the gift of Matrimony,
> they may be known for the integrity of their conduct
> (and be recognized as virtuous parents).
>
> In happiness may they praise you, O Lord,
> in sorrow may they seek you out;
> may they have the joy of your presence
> to assist them in their toil,
> and know that you are near
> to comfort them in their need;
> and after a happy old age,

together with the circle of friends that surrounds them,
may they come to the Kingdom of Heaven.
Through Christ our Lord.
R. Amen.

Then the priest or deacon blesses the people, saying:
May almighty God bless all of you,
who are gathered here,
the Father, and the Son, ✝ and the Holy Spirit.
R. Amen.

Appendixes

A. Marriage between a Catholic and a Non-Catholic

The Catholic Church believes that marriage between one man and one woman is a natural institution; that is, it is woven into the very fabric of what it means to be part and parcel of the human family and reflects God's plan for that family. When these two people are baptized Christians, this natural institution of marriage becomes a sacrament. In other words, because each person shares in the life of the Holy Spirit and discipleship to Jesus, their whole life together becomes a vibrant, visible sign of the invisible reality of God's unending love for the world. Marriage brings the couple God's rich blessing of grace, and the couple becomes a medium of God's grace to others.

It is quite common, of course, for a Catholic to marry a member of a different Christian tradition. For example, many Catholics marry Methodists, Lutherans, Episcopalians, members of nondenominational communities, or Christians who for one reason or another remain unaffiliated with a particular faith community. Other Catholics marry someone who has never been baptized. The person may be Jewish, Muslim, Hindu, Buddhist, or unaffiliated with any faith. Keep in mind that whether a Catholic enters into a sacramental marriage with a Christian of a different church or a valid marriage with a non-Christian, the Church supports the witness of love and fidelity the couple offers to the world.

During the course of your marriage preparation, issues of faith and belief should be addressed in an open and honest way, both about the faith you share and the significant differences in what you believe and how you practice your religious faith. Speaking candidly about these issues with the priest or deacon helping you prepare for your marriage is very important.

A Pastoral Note on Intercommunion

One of the most sensitive and easily misunderstood issues in Catholic life and practice today is the prohibition of intercommunion—the reception of Holy Communion in the Catholic Church by non-Catholics or its reception by Catholics in other Christian churches. Some Catholics who have a non-Catholic fiancé, family members, or friends may believe that an injustice is being done and that Catholic limitations on intercommunion are contrary to the gospels' teaching of love and acceptance. Why, then, are non-Catholics asked not to take Communion at Mass?

The reasons behind the Catholic prohibition of intercommunion are not based on a perceived moral or religious superiority of Catholics over other Christians. There are many faithful members of other Christian traditions who are morally or religiously better Christians than nominal Catholics, but that is not what is at stake in intercommunion. The Catholic discipline of not practicing intercommunion is based on a theology of the Eucharist: what it is, what it does, and what it signifies.

Many Christian denominations do not share our Catholic understanding of the Eucharist. Some view communion as a rich symbol and a memorial of what Jesus has done for us, but for Catholics, the Eucharist is more than a memorial meal. It makes real again all of the power and promise of Christ's life-giving death and resurrection. Catholics believe that the Eucharist is a sacrament and therefore a particular kind of sign that effects or brings about what it signifies. In essence, we believe that Holy Communion doesn't just *point us* to the presence of Christ but that—through a profound mystery—it *is* the presence of Christ, which we consume in order to better become that divine presence in the world.

But these differences regarding what Holy Communion is are not the sole obstacle to intercommunion. There is also the matter of what Holy Communion does. Catholics believe that the Eucharist draws those who receive Communion into greater unity within the Body of Christ and at the same time signifies that unity. The Eucharist, simply put, is both a sign and source of unity in the Church. Thus, the Eucharist is not only about uniting individual believers to Christ through a share in Communion but more fundamentally about uniting a community of believers together. When one receives Communion, he or she is saying yes to a communion of mind and heart with the Church. It is an act that signifies not only a spiritual union with other members of the Church but also a public affirmation of being united in the beliefs and practices of that community.

The reception of Holy Communion by members of another Christian denomination cannot be a sign of unity among those believers when, in fact, significant differences in belief and practice still remain between Catholics and those of other Christian churches. Eucharistic communion would then be a counter-sign: it would signify a unity that does not exist among these Christians. Given all of this, while it is certainly not prohibited for couples to use the Order of Celebrating Matrimony within Mass when one partner is a baptized non-Catholic, it may be better to use the second form of the celebrations, the Order of Celebrating Matrimony without Mass in order to avoid misunderstanding or insult.

This appendix is also available at TogetherforLifeOnline.com.

B. Honoring Ethnic and Cultural Traditions

A child eating with her mother and grandmother asked, "Mom, why do you always cut an inch off the end of the Thanksgiving ham?" The mother replied, "I learned that from your grandmother. It makes the ham juicier. Right, Mama?" The grandmother giggled: "I did it because I didn't have a roasting pan big enough!"

Some say tradition is an excuse to act without thinking. When it comes to rituals, whether religious or secular, we often simply do what we've seen and learned from others. But not knowing where our traditions come from can lead us to do some strange things that may not fit our own situation.

The same is true when preparing a wedding. You might be surprised to know that a lot of what you see and hear on television or in the movies or even at the last Catholic wedding you attended isn't actually part of *The Order of Celebrating Matrimony*. Some examples of these customs include the bride walking down the aisle by herself, improvised or customized vows, lighting a unity candle, pouring sand into a vase, or placing flowers at an image of Mary.

If these aren't in the Catholic rite, where did they come from? Why do some Catholic weddings have them? And how do you know which of these would be appropriate for your wedding?

Something Old

Some of these traditions come from a time and culture in which marriage was treated as a contract between families and the transfer of wealth and property played an important role. "Giving away the bride" ritualized this contract. In this light, you can see how the tradition of the father escorting his daughter to her groom may have developed. Catholics, however, believe that the bride and groom give themselves to each other as equal partners, and as one, they give themselves to God. Does this mean it would be inappropriate to follow this tradition? Not necessarily. Parents play a major role in our lives, and sharing this moment with them is a gift. But there are ways to blend tradition with what the rite requests. For example, the groom might walk in first with his parents, followed by the bride with hers. Or parents can process in together followed by the wedding party with bride and groom together at the end. Discussing these options with your family and parish ministers might also give you some valuable time to reflect on the role your family has had in your relationship and may help mend divisions.

Something New

Some traditions are actually trends in popular culture. These include customs like the unity candle, a sand ceremony, or improvised vows. These practices developed relatively recently and have been used in both religious and civil ceremonies. Of these, the unity candle is most popular, but it is not required and technically not allowed to be used during Catholic weddings.

Lighting candles, however, does have great significance in the Catholic Church. Our most important candle is the Paschal or Easter Candle, which is first lit each year at the Easter Vigil and remains prominent throughout the Easter season. All the candles given at infant and adult baptisms are lit from this candle. It is also lit during funerals to mark our loved one's passage to eternal life. We honor the Paschal Candle because it represents Christ, the Light.

One reason the Church's rite does not include a unity candle may be that its popular meaning—two lives becoming one—is already profoundly signified through the couple's exchange of vows and rings and in the nuptial blessing. Some churches allow a unity candle to be lit after the conclusion of the rite, just before the recessional.

If you are both baptized (even if in another Christian tradition) and permitted to incorporate a unity candle at the end of your wedding, you might light your smaller candles from the Paschal Candle and, using them, light your unity candle. Don't blow out your own smaller candles—your identity does not disappear when you get married; it is shared and transformed into something new, a third reality represented by the unity candle. Another custom in some places is to light a unity candle to formally open the wedding reception. For an example of how to do this, visit TogetherforLifeOnline.com.

Something Borrowed

Other traditions are rooted in our ethnic cultures. These customs hold deep meaning for many families, and the Church invites couples to include them in their ceremony if they do not conflict with a Christian understanding of marriage. For example, in many Hispanic families, there is a blessing and giving of coins; Filipino families place a *lazo* or veil and a cord over the couple; Vietnamese couples honor their ancestors; and Celtic families wear the colors of their clan. Additional information about ethnic wedding traditions and how to adapt them to *The Order of Celebrating Matrimony* and the liturgical norms of the Catholic Church are available at TogetherforLifeOnline.com.

Something Blue

Finally, some of our traditions developed from a spiritual devotion to the Virgin Mary. She is a model for living one's faith in the good and bad of everyday life. It is natural, then, for Catholics to want to pray to her as they begin their new life together. Some couples place flowers at an image of Mary and spend a few moments in prayer to her during the wedding. But more often than not, couples really just want a special song sung at that time, and they may think they need to take flowers to a statue of Mary in order to have that song included. Not so. If both of you genuinely have a devotion to Mary, then certainly ask if you can include this tradition. But if it is not allowed, keep in mind that you are not required to do it.

Ritual traditions take root in our lives most often because they unite us to the past, connect to who we are today, and help us express who we want to become. Good rituals are powerful because they communicate this connection clearly. As you prepare your wedding, look first at the traditions that have been handed on to you from all the cultures that make you who you are today. Especially begin with the rite from our ancestors in the faith. Explore where these traditions come from and what they mean. Adapt them for your wedding with the help of your parish staff so they express what the two of you hope for in your married life.

For more on ethnic and cultural traditions, visit TogetherforLifeOnline.com.

Contributors

Ann M. Garrido, DMin, is associate professor of homiletics at Aquinas Institute of Theology in St. Louis, Missouri. She is the author of five books, including *Redeeming Conflict* and the award-winning *Redeeming Administration.*

Msgr. Michael Heintz, PhD, is a priest of the Diocese of Fort Wayne–South Bend, rector of St. Matthew Cathedral in South Bend, Indiana, and director of the master of divinity program at the University of Notre Dame.

Diana Macalintal, MA, is the director of worship for the diocese of San Jose, cofounder of TeamRCIA.com, and author of three books including, *The Work of Your Hands* and *Joined by the Church, Sealed by a Blessing.*

H. Richard McCord, EdD, served as executive director for the Secretariat of Laity, Marriage, Family Life and Youth at the United States Conference of Catholic Bishops from 1998 to 2011.

Geoffrey D. Miller, PhD, is assistant professor of biblical studies at Saint Louis University and an expert on the book of Tobit.

Tim Muldoon, PhD, is assistant to the vice president for University Mission and Ministry at Boston College. He was the inaugural director of the Church in the 21st Century Center at Boston College from 2005 to 2007.

Julie Hanlon Rubio, PhD, is professor of Christian ethics at Saint Louis University, where she has taught courses in marriage, sexual ethics, religion and politics, and social justice since 1999.

Deacon William F. Urbine, DMin, is assistant director of the Office of the Permanent Diaconate and served as director of the Office of Family Life Ministries for the diocese of Allentown, Pennsylvania, from 2000 to 2011.

Peter A. Jarret, C.S.C., is superior and rector of Moreau Seminary at the University of Notre Dame. He was born in Providence, Rhode Island, and graduated from the University of Notre Dame in 1986, entering the Congregation of Holy Cross the following year. Ordained a Holy Cross priest in April 1992, he served several years at Christ the King Parish in South Bend, Indiana, and then as pastor of St. Pius X Parish in Granger, Indiana, for six years. Following five years as rector in an undergraduate residence hall and counselor to the university president, Rev. Edward Malloy, C.S.C., he was then appointed religious superior with ministerial responsibility for nearly eighty Holy Cross religious at Notre Dame from 2006 to 2010. Jarret is a contributor to *The Cross, Our Only Hope*; *The Gift of the Cross*; *The Gift of Hope*; and *The Notre Dame Book of Prayer*.

Msgr. Joseph M. Champlin (1930–2008) served in sacramental ministry as resident priest at Our Lady of Good Counsel in Warners, New York. He was the former rector of the Cathedral of the Immaculate Conception in his home diocese of Syracuse. A prolific writer on a variety of pastoral care and spirituality concerns and traveled more than two million miles lecturing in the United States and abroad. Among his more than fifty books are *Slow Down* and *Take Five* from Sorin Books; and *Should We Marry?*, *From the Heart*, *Together for Life*, and *Through Death to Life* from Ave Maria Press.

SELECTION FORM for the readings, prayers and blessings to be used in the liturgy.

Also available at **togetherforlifeonline.com**

_____   _____
Groom   Phone

_____   _____
Bride   Phone

_____   _____
Priest or Deacon   Church

_____   _____
Date of Celebration   Time

_____
Best Man

_____
Maid or Matron of Honor

_____   _____
Rehearsal Date   Time

_____   _____
Number of Ushers / Greeters   Number of Bridesmaids / Groomsmen

Ring Bearer: _____   _____
                    YES   NO

Flower Girl(s):   _____   _____   _____
                    YES   NO   HOW MANY?

Music Director   Other
Contacted: _____   _____   Musicians: _____   _____
                YES   NO   YES   NO

Altar
Servers: WE WILL PROVIDE _____   HAVE CHURCH PROVIDE _____

Which form of celebrating matrimony?

_____ (1) Within Mass

_____ (2) Without Mass

_____ (3) Between a Catholic and Catechumen or Non-Christian

Indicate your selections in the proper spaces and return this form to the priest, deacon, or other parish staff person helping you plan your wedding. This selection form is also available at togetherforlifeonline.com

Entrance Procession: (check or fill in)

_____ Both bride and groom accompanied by parents, preceded by bridesmaids, groomsmen, and presiding clergy

_____ Both bride and groom accompanied by parents, preceded by bridesmaids and groomsmen

_____ Bride accompanied by parents, preceded by bridesmaids and groomsmen

_____ Bride accompanied by father, preceded by bridesmaids and groomsmen

_____ Other:_____

_____

Collect: pages 11–13 (A1–A6)

No._____ , page _____

Old Testament Reading: pages 16–33 (B1–B9)

No._____ , page _____

Read by_____

Responsorial Psalm: pages 36–41 (C1–C7)

No._____ , page _____

Sung or read by_____

New Testament Reading: pages 44–66 (D1–D14)

No._____ , page _____

Read by_____

Alleluia Verse and Verse before the Gospel: page 70 (E1–E6)

No. _____ Sung _____

Gospel Reading: pages 72–86 (F1–F10)

No. _____ , page _____

Read by Presiding Priest or Deacon

The Celebration of Matrimony

The Questions before the Consent: pages 88–90

_____ G1   _____ G2   _____ G3

The Consent: pages 90–92 (H1–H12)

No. _____ , page _____

Reception of the consent: pages 92–93

____ H13a   ____ H13b   ____ H14a   ____ H14b   ____ H15a   ____ H15b

Blessing and Giving of Rings: page 93–94 (I1–I5)

No. _____ , page _____

Blessing and Giving of the *Arras*: page 95

_____ I6   _____ I7   _____ I8

Universal Prayer: pages 95–97 (J1–J2),

No. _____ , page _____

Read by _____

Personally composed _____ Prepared by priest/deacon _____

If you are not celebrating Mass, skip to Nuptial Blessing.

Presentation of the Gifts:

Brought forward by: _____

Gift for the poor: Yes ____   No ____

Total number of persons bringing up gifts _____

Prayer over the Offerings: pages 98–99 (K1–K3)

No._____, page _____

Preface: pages 99–101 (L1–L3)

No._____, page _____

Blessing and Placing of the *Lazo* or the Veil: pages 102, 111 (M)

No._____, page_____

Nuptial Blessing: pages 102–106 (M1–M3), page 111–113 (M5)

No._____, page_____

If you are not celebrating Mass, skip to Final Blessing.

Communion: (Who in the immediate wedding party who will receive communion)

Groom _____   Bride_____

Maid or Matron of Honor _____   Best Man _____

Under both kinds: Yes _____   No _____

Prayer after Communion: page 107 (N1–N3)

No. _____, page_____

Final or Solemn Blessing: pages 108–110 (O1–O3)

No. _____,_ page _____

Other Special Elements in Our Ceremony:

_____

_____

_____

Note: The parish music director should be helpful in designing a ceremony that will include congregational singing. A participation booklet, described elsewhere in this volume, can aid in fostering such involvement by the guests present.

TOGETHER *for* LIFE *online*

Get more wedding planning help at

togetherforlifeonline.com

At *Together for Life Online* You'll Find:

- Ideas and tips for planning your Catholic wedding
- Quality resources to help strengthen your marriage
- Marriage enrichment opportunities
- A Catholic wedding planning checklist with a timeline and tasks

You can also find the *Together for Life* selection form at togetherforlifeonline.com/selectionform

AVE

AVE MARIA PRESS